1999

Believing the Creed

Believing the Creed

A Metaphorical Approach

John Ogden

British Library Cataloguing in Publication data
A catalogue record for this book is available
from the British Library

978 0 7162 0657 6

This edition published 2009
by Epworth Press
Methodist Church House
25 Marylebone Road
London NW1 5JR.

Typeset by Regent Typesetting, London
Printed and bound in Great Britain by
CPI Antony Rowe, Chippenham SN14 6LH

Contents

To the memory of two Methodist Ministers:
my grandfather, Harold Ogden, who set me off on my faith-journey,
and Alan Elgar, who taught me to ask questions

Acknowledgements

In the course of writing this book I have read a number of others. While these are mentioned in the text and listed at the end, it is right that at this point I acknowledge particular debts to other writers. Frances Young[1] has provided a stimulating – even exciting – tour of controversies in the early Church and their influence on the shape of the creeds. David Harned[2] gives a perspective on the Apostles' Creed in terms of personal commitment. In the work of the late D. Z. Phillips[3] I found a most helpful contribution to the heart-rending questions about believing in the love of God in the face of the wretchedness of the human condition – and to much more besides.

For the opportunity to be involved as a Local Tutor in the Southern Theological Education and Training Scheme (STETS), I will always be grateful; this experience has been stimulating beyond measure. A Clergy Study Break at Sarum College in the autumn of 2007 provided the stimulus for a significant leap forward. I am grateful to the Reading and Silchester Circuit of the Methodist Church which allowed me a brief sabbatical and funded that short visit. I am conscious also of my debt to the friends who have read partial drafts of the text as it evolved, and whose comments have both sobered and sustained my enthusiasm. Finally, I owe a particular debt to Revd Dr Angela Shier-Jones, who has

1 Frances M. Young, *The Making of the Creeds*, London, SCM Press, 2002.

2 D. B. Harned, *Creed and Personal Identity: The Meaning of the Apostles' Creed*, Philadelphia, Fortress Press, 1981.

3 D. Z. Phillips, *The Problem of Evil and the Problem of God*, London, SCM Press, 2004.

been my shepherd over several months; without her patient help, this book would have for ever remained sprawling and unfocused on my hard drive. The quirks and faults of presentation, however, remain my responsibility alone.

Introduction

When my wife and I visit her sister in North Lincolnshire there's a bend in the road, at the top of a slight rise, which marks the beginning of the end of our journey. Within minutes we shall arrive, glad of a rest after the better part of four hours (plus coffee breaks) on the road. This particular bend is visible from a distance, because there is always some item of farm machinery parked in the adjoining field right at the corner; there are no hedges, because this is arable land. Each time we pass it, I wonder about this piece of machinery. How long has it been left there? Is it in fact the same one we saw the last time we were here? What was it used for? Is it just parked there when not required? Or is it now a neglected ruin, no longer capable of being refurbished and put to use?

I sometimes think of the Creed[1] like that: a piece of discarded machinery that we pass by quite frequently. And the Creed prompts a range of questions that are not unlike the questions I ask myself about the farm machinery at the bend on the slight rise.

The cover picture of this book is found among the splendid images of deep space created using the Hubble Telescope. It is particularly appropriate for a book like this. Why? Space offers no footholds and no built-in frame of reference, even when the mission is close to our own planet. Venturing into *really* deep space will present greater conceptual challenges. The astronaut of such a distant future will be able to look around her and say:

1 In general we refer to 'The Creed', meaning the Apostles' Creed. In fact, as we shall see, there are others. Arguably we might have chosen to use the phrase 'the creeds' or perhaps 'credal formulations' to embrace them all. While our remarks are indeed about a wider class of credal formulations, the approach is initially via a single creed.

'Somewhere out there, in some direction or other, is a tiny planet, Earth, and on that planet lie the familiar hills, lakes, meadows and woodlands of my home. There I could stand on solid ground and know without a shadow of doubt which way was "up" and which way was "down". Out here there is no horizon, no up and no down, no handgrip, no lifeline.'

People exploring the Christian faith for the first time may well feel a bit like an astronaut. Whatever frame of reference they bring to the party seems to make no sense. Perhaps that is why many go away completely baffled. Possibly the same is true for some committed Christians as they join in the recital of the Creed during worship.

But the notion of space calls to mind also the theme of liberation. John Gillespie Magee was a fighter pilot in the Second World War. He wrote a short poem entitled 'High Flight', which was quoted by President Ronald Reagan after the *Challenger* disaster of 28 January 1986. The poem began: 'Oh! I have slipped the surly bonds of Earth', and ended with the words, 'I have . . . put out my hand, and touched the face of God'.

This book sets out to create a space for belief by dispelling the notion that to say the Creed is to be subject to intolerable intellectual shackles; it is to claim that one believes the impossible. Our approach is to view the Creed as a collection of metaphors, which together tell a symbolic story. To some readers this may seem strange – a bit like denying that the Creed has anything to say that can ring true for us. We will try to recognize the hazards implicit in attempting to take the Creed literally, and negotiate those hazards safely – negotiate in the sense of 'avoid'. But 'negotiate' has another meaning: having a conversation with another party, recognizing that each will be changed by the experience; neither is 'immovable, infixt and frozen round'.[2] The conversational encounter is what really matters. And its outcome is always provisional (as St Paul remarked at the end of his celebrated Hymn to Love, in chapter 13 of his first letter to Christians in Corinth). Through this conversation we are liberated, set free to be ourselves. We shall, I hope, discover space to believe.

2 John Milton, *Paradise Lost*, II, line 602.

Before going any further, I need to add that for me – as for many others – the historic creeds are a vital part of our Christian heritage. While those of us who are Christians must always interpret our belief against the background of changing times, it would in my view be wrong to play down the importance of these historic documents. I shall return to this later.

When Christians are invited to join together in saying the Creed, many of us have difficulties with one or more of its clauses. We are perhaps conditioned to be a bit ashamed of our doubts, and so we ask ourselves whether our reservations about this or that proposition require us to remain silent at that particular point in the recital, or to remain silent during the Creed, or – more radical still – to stay away from church altogether. Professor Keith Ward writes of this problem of saying the Creed.[3] On those occasions when I invite congregations to say a Creed, I suggest that they stand alongside the whole Church in its ongoing search for meaning and truth, of which the text before them is but one staging post. This is the ongoing process of negotiation to which I referred above.

Given that I am a Methodist, and British Methodists don't say the Creed in church very often, you may wonder why I have written this book. My answer, of course, is that there is much more to it than what is going on in our heads when we say the Creed together. If in our churches we are not encouraged to raise questions about the Creed, we may feel a degree of doubt, a lack of confidence in our understanding of the Christian faith. This is not a good starting-point from which to embark on a conversation with anyone – fellow church member or not.

Likewise, there are, I suspect, people outside or on the margins of the Church for whom all this emphasis on believing is a real problem. At some time the Creed has been presented to them as a kind of ultimatum: believe this . . . or else! They are given no clue about the ways in which to negotiate with the Creed and use it as a way of exploring the faith they already have. Nor are they always aware of the number of people within the Church who share their difficulties at least enough to have a meaningful conversation with them about the faith they share (or don't share).

---

3 K. Ward, *A Vision to Pursue*, SCM Press, 1991, pp. 1–11.

So, my hope is that this book will encourage people to 'lighten up' in relation to the Creed, to use it as the point of departure for a serious expedition into the world of their own faith and that of their own community. In that last sentence I hesitated about the phrase 'point of departure'. Should I not be encouraging people to see the Creed more as a map; go to this place and this is what you will find; turn right just here and you will come safely home again? It cannot be denied that this may be a valid and helpful way of looking at it. But I want to claim that this is not the only way, or even – for many people – the most helpful, particularly in times when even the notion of believing is itself subject to unsettling change.

We need to raise another group of questions about how we believe. For some, there is only one possible answer to such questions: when I say 'I believe *X*' I mean simply that *X* is the case. For example, if I say: 'Ben Nevis is the highest mountain in the UK', I mean that there is in fact no higher mountain in the UK – a claim that a competent surveyor could confirm. But there are other issues around believing, and in some circumstances that particular one – of correspondence with the facts – might not be the most important. It may be reassuring to know *X* with absolute certainty, but our grasp of what *X* really *means* might change with our circumstances – or simply as we grow older.

As we grow older, our ways of responding to the world around us change, and that includes our response to faith, our need for faith and the kind of faith we need. Many people have remarked on the fact that young people's relationship with their parents doesn't fully mature until they have flown the nest, found themselves, and come back as friends. Far too many people have rejected Christianity as adults because they are stuck with a picture of it that is suitable only for a small child; after all, it's what they were taught in Sunday School. They need to discover for themselves a grown-up faith that matches the way they really are at the age of 35 or 47 or 64 or 79. Perhaps they need to come back to God as a friend. Perhaps they even need to let God grow up (in their minds).

Finally (for the present), there is an underlying question about whether 'believing' is in any case the point of the story. How important is it to the Christian faith that you believe (whatever that word might mean) certain rather abstract propositions about God, Jesus etc.? It does rather suggest that our admission to heaven will be a bit like a basic oral examination on 'the facts', a picture which is utterly different from the one that Jesus painted. So, if believing is not the most important aspect of being a Christian, what is? We shall have reason later on to discuss *believing* alongside three other 'b' words: *belonging*, *behaving* and *becoming*. And if believing continues to have a place for Christians, what might that place be?

Of course people's hesitations about the Christian faith aren't only about what to believe. There are many other issues too, issues that could be addressed and are addressed by other books. This book doesn't attempt to compete with them. My aim in writing about Christian believing is to see whether there is a way of working with it that can engage the interest and even the excitement of many more people. Is it possible, for example, for the Creed to be a way of understanding the perplexities of human existence, while remaining a body of worthwhile and distinctively Christian belief? In a word, my hope and passionate desire is to find an alternative to two extremes: on the one hand out-and-out dismissal of the Creed; and on the other, its total uncritical acceptance at face value. My belief is that this alternative will offer rich rewards to people who are perplexed about the place of faith in their lives and their world.

Inevitably, a focus upon the Creed creates a difficulty, which challenges both those who find it baffling and those who hold it in reverence. It suggests that what you believe (in the '*X* is the case' sense) is all that matters about Christianity. For many, this is a huge obstacle to understanding what faith is all about. So, although this book started life as a series of reflections on the Apostles' Creed, it has carried me far beyond, into a discussion about what the word 'to believe' means; about the really important things the Creed doesn't say about being a Christian.

So, what am I aiming to do in this book? Clearly, since that's where it began its life, I want to look at the Creed – specifically the Apostles' Creed – as a convenient 'way in' to questions about believing. But before we embark on that specific task, we spend some time, in Part 1, trying to evaluate how our culture expresses and conveys meaning, in terms of metaphor, myth and story.

The Creed, however, falls far short of being a comprehensive account of what it means to be a member of the Christian faith-tradition. On the face of it, the Creed isn't even a primary source; surely that privilege belongs to the Bible. Moreover, the teaching found in the Bible (like that which has been condensed into the Creed) has undergone a process of development over the centuries as Christians have tried faithfully and courageously to live their lives in the light of these sources to which they are heirs. That process of development, of course, took place as the circumstances in the world changed, in terms of political, social and cultural influences. Christians have always tried to live their faith 'in the real world' as they understood it (that real world) to be; at the same time they feel deeply committed to the whole Christian story as it first took written form, as it has been understood over the centuries, and as they themselves are struggling to make sense of it in their own present context.

In recent centuries the gulf between faith and its cultural setting has become very wide – so wide that many find it hard to hold a faith of any kind while struggling with the challenges of the real world. One specific challenge they face is that – certainly in popular understanding – faith is unprovable, while the real world is (or claims to be) concerned with that which can be proved. But is this a fair reflection of the real world? Is it a fair reflection of what it means to have faith?

One of the fascinating features of that journey of the centuries is the varying ways in which Christian people have actually worked with the text of scripture. Many twenty-first-century Christians might be astonished at the ways in which scripture has been appropriated and used in times past; they might also be bewildered to learn, for example, that the idea of a strictly literal interpretation of scripture is a comparatively recent development. It was born out of a kind of rearguard action, in order to find and defend a corner in which faith might take shelter from the onslaught of modernity.

In considering some examples from this journey of the centuries, we shall discover that the choice before us is far more subtle than we might suppose. It is not a stark choice between, on the one hand, believing the Bible literally, and on the other dismissing Bible and Creed as outdated fairy-tales. It is as if we were examining a photographic image of the Bible using the kind of computer software with which we might adjust our digital photos in various ways. The choice is not between monochrome (black-and-white) and sepia; there is an immense range of colours available. Contrast, brightness and saturation can be adjusted too, and the brilliance of the original can be brought to life. The truth of these original texts does not lie in their literal truth, but in the change that comes about in us when we are touched deeply by what they have to say.

Perhaps, at risk of too many analogies, it may be permissible to introduce one more. The late Alfred Wainwright wrote a wonderful series of books about the fells of the English Lake District. Handwritten, and illustrated by many hand-drawn sketches of routes and views, fell-walkers love these books and turn to them time and again for guidance and inspiration. Over the years since Wainwright first created these books, some features of the landscape have changed – in most cases only very slightly. The books can indeed serve as guide and inspiration, but the experience of each walk is new. A walker today will see much that Wainwright would have seen, and much that he could not have seen. The changing quality of light ensures that every new walk is a revelation.

I would like to suggest that the Creed – and all that it stands for – shares something of the characteristics of Wainwright's books. Delightful and informative on the shelf and in the home, their best use is to encourage readers to walk, to see for themselves, and make the experience of faith their own.

The book begins with a section (Part 1: 'The Context of Believing') devoted to looking at the context in which people live today. That is in fact an impossibly grandiose claim. Within the compass of one modest book a comprehensive survey would be out of the question. We concentrate here on the world of ideas and how they play out in various aspects of contemporary life. There is also a chapter on the various ways in which we use language, and how this has a bearing on the way we understand religious language.

Part 2 ('The Content of Believing') is based on the Apostles' Creed. It does not claim to be an exhaustive treatment of this vast subject, but rather attempts to draw together some of the key ideas that underlie the Creed, from the perspective of a Christian believer.

Part 3 ('Believing in Context') begins with a pause for breath (Chapter 8) in which we ask where our study of the Creed leaves us. We then explore some matters central to Christian self-understanding about which the Creed is entirely silent. We consider here topics such as grace, covenant and discipleship, as well as touching upon some of the tough questions about why bad things happen to good people. Part 3 then returns to the contemporary world, revisiting some of the issues raised in Part 1 and elsewhere in the light of what we have learned about the content of believing. The Appendix also includes a short discussion of the numerous modern creed-like statements of faith.

Part 1

The Context of Believing

Our first exploratory ventures will be into the world around us, the world of our daily newspapers, TV and radio news bulletins, current affairs and technology. For good or ill this is the world that sets the agenda. Its inhabitants are the movers and shakers, the trendsetters, the arbiters of popular culture. To a large extent they shape our thinking. In part, this atmosphere guides us positively in directing us what to think. It also guides us – or attempts to guide us – negatively by ruling out certain ideas. This happens through the voices of derision and denial as well as those of direct prohibition. Unfavoured ideas are at best studiously ignored; they get no air time, no thoughtful discussion, so we never get the chance to evaluate them properly. Quite frequently they are treated with utter disdain.

This is the context in which the voices of faith try to be heard. Some of these voices are loud and strident; some are angry, impatient, even violent; others take a different approach. Before we make up our minds, we need to understand the context in which the life of faith is being lived right now. In the first part of this book, that is our goal. Our investigation will range over a number (but by no means an exhaustive number) of unlikely-sounding topics, trying to identify points of contention and points of possible agreement. If there is to be debate, even disagreement, let it be courteous, based on an honest and serious attempt to understand where people are coming from.

The treatment given here is inevitably partial, based on the author's experience and interests. Readers are encouraged to look with equally critical eyes on the world as they themselves see it.

One of the features of the modern world is the diversity of the ways in which we use language. Language is a primary tool of human discourse, and in exploring it we hope to create a toolkit for the remainder of our inquiry. We begin, therefore, with a look at language itself and the various ways in which it is used, giving particular attention to indirect patterns of use in religious language as such, trying to identify possible reactions to it, and our own responses to those reactions. We shall then turn to the Bible and explore how language is used there – or rather, how our understanding of language can help us understand the Bible.

In Chapter 2 we examine the way in which religious language works, and the responses it evokes from various quarters, including especially the world of science. Our final port of call in Chapter 2 is the contentious issue of postmodernism.

In Chapter 3 we look at the idea of story and its relationship with truth, first in the world of science, then, briefly, in the novel, and finally as a possible basis for engaging with the Creed.

I

The Language We Use

We use language every day, of course, when we write letters, prepare shopping lists, and in the chit-chat with the person at the supermarket checkout. We listen to the radio and watch television. The language of the 'sit-com', however, is very different from the language of the news bulletin, the political commentary, the biographical interview, the travel programme or the scientific documentary. We read newspapers and occasionally novels. Look carefully, however, and you will find that the language of newspapers is different from that of the novel. One newspaper will read very differently from another. Every day we encounter a particular style of language known as 'advertising copy', language designed to persuade you that the product or service being advertised is 'simply unmissable'.

We are bombarded with language every day. Many of us will have no difficulty in recognizing the difference between one style and another, and will be able to change gear mentally in response. It has become so natural that we hardly even think about it. In the ways in which we communicate with one another we have acquired the skill of knowing what kind of language is suitable for one purpose, and how that is different from the kind of language appropriate for another. We would not, for example, think of writing a job application in the language of the text message. A news bulletin played for laughs, in the language and style of a comedian, would startle us and probably cause real offence. Furthermore, we wouldn't know whether to take its content seriously.

In short, the way in which language is used – the way the ideas are packaged and delivered – can be very significant in how successful it is as a communication between people. To 'get the message' we need to know and understand the way in which the message is being packaged for us, as well as understand the meanings of the words.

It's a bit like learning a foreign language – more than matching a succession of words in our own language with the corresponding word in another language. People who have successfully made the transition to living in France sometimes say, 'I've learned to think in French.' In Italian there's a saying, '*traduttore, traditore*', which in English means: 'translator, you are a traitor'. In other words, it is not possible to express in any other language the subtleties of mood and nuance that come naturally in one's mother tongue.

In conversation with a friend, we may imagine that, because we are both using a given collection of words, we are in fact using them in the same way. Often this is not so. The academic discipline of philosophy is in part concerned with clarifying the way we use words, so that when people think they are discussing the same thing, they are absolutely clear about the different ways they use words to express their meaning.

This is hard enough when we are in face-to-face conversation with another living person. Imagine the challenge, then, of trying to get to grips with a document written hundreds or even thousands of years ago. Those who wrote it are no less human than we are, no less capable of profound and insightful thought. How do we know – how can we know – what lies behind their use of language? If I am a scientist, or a lawyer, a building surveyor or a bricklayer, a poet or a policeman, a journalist or a sales manager, I will bring to my task the habits formed by my own use of language. How can such a diverse group of people approach this daunting task with any hope that something worthwhile might emerge? Scholars may be able to supply informed guesses about how language was used in long-forgotten centuries, but certainty is beyond our grasp. We must enter into conversation with this ancient text – or rather with the minds that shaped it. In doing so, we need to appreciate the range of possibilities before us as we try to grasp what the text might mean for us.

Here are some simple examples of what I mean by the diversity of language. Sometimes the language we use is all very factual: 'I'll have four medium slices of that ham, please', or 'Do you have this dress in any other colour?' At other times it's much more expressive: 'You know, our Darren's always been in a bit of a dream; well he seems to be getting worse.' Or perhaps: 'Did you see last night's sunset? The sky was ablaze!' In these last two examples a real thing or person was described using language that couldn't possibly be taken literally – but we have no difficulty in understanding what was meant. It helps, of course, that what we're talking about is itself real, not just a figment of our imagination.

The language we're using here – of dreamy Darren or blazing sunsets – is that of metaphor, a way of talking indirectly about something or someone because we find it the most effective way of saying what we want to say. No one imagines that the sky at sunset is actually on fire; it's just that to describe it as being ablaze says exactly what we want to say about it. Words may exist that could describe the sunset more directly. A physicist, for example, might be able to talk about the absorption of light of particular frequencies giving rise to a sky that looks brilliant orange. His description might be more accurate (in some senses) but no one would want to describe the sunset in this way in a letter to a close friend who happened to be an artist.

We need to explore this indirect kind of language before we plunge into the Creed itself. In doing so, we need to consider a much more serious difficulty. We've talked so far about things, or people, that are real; we're been choosing the right kind of language in the light of what it is we want to say about them. We could say other things about them for which a completely different sort of language would be appropriate: 'Darren is six feet tall', or 'The sunset lasted for eleven minutes.' Perhaps what we are doing, with the 'Darren is a dream' language, is describing our reactions to them, our impressions of them, rather than the things or people themselves.

Suppose, however, that what we wanted to describe or talk about is utterly different, so different that we don't have access to any other, more direct language at all for talking about them; so different, in fact, that we cannot even answer the question, 'Does it exist?' The only language at our command for describing what we are experiencing, or believing, is this indirect, metaphoric language.

Mystery

Here we must introduce another idea: mystery. For most of us, a mystery is a puzzle for which we believe there is a solution; it's just that we haven't yet found that solution. Some years ago, before going on holiday, I put something I particularly treasured (it was a fountain pen) in a safe place in my study. Unfortunately I didn't make a note of where that safe place was. I've never seen that treasured pen since. Where has it gone? It's a complete mystery. That is one use of the word 'mystery': a puzzle that has a solution we haven't yet discovered.

There is of course another meaning of 'mystery' – it is an idea or proposition for which there is no known test, nor will there ever be such a test. Yet we remain convinced that this 'thing' does exist, this notion is in some sense true, even though we can't prove it and we don't even have language for talking about it. Once again we're in the realm of impressions, feelings, inner responses, rather than 'facts on the ground'.

Within Christian history there have been two ways of using the word 'mystery'. From the Greek world of the first century we find the so-called mystery religions. These were about secret knowledge, revealed only to the initiated. From the specifically Christian world the word 'mystery' has a more specialized meaning. It refers to the story of a set of communities who saw themselves as God's people, a story in which (so they believed) the hand of God was at work, planning the birth and ministry of Jesus from the beginning of time. Today, in services of Holy Communion, many Christians recite a simple formula known (somewhat mysteriously) as the 'mystery of faith': 'Christ has died; Christ is risen; Christ will come again'. We may find it completely impossible to attach ordinary meanings to these words, but somehow for Christians what they express is close to the heart of what we believe.

Metaphor in today's world

For most of my life I taught computer science in a university. My colleagues and I were concerned with processes that take place in a computer, manipulating information stored in a computer's memory. For most of us, the objective was to enable ordinary people to make constructive use of the computer. But what goes on inside a computer can be described in many ways. At the finest level of detail these processes involve the movement of electrons in semiconductors under very small forces which change very rapidly. Described at this level, even a very simple task like keeping track of the time would involve immense quantities of information. Directing such a task using commands appropriate to this level of description would be akin to herding locusts. Change the computational scale from the very simple to the immensely complex, to something like modelling the weather, and both the description and the control would rapidly become unimaginably complex and difficult.

In computing, the answer to this problem is to organize the computer in such a way that the processes and the information can be described in terms that make sense to a mathematician or engineer rather than to a computer hardware specialist. This is achieved by a means similar to the management of any very large organization: hierarchy and delegation. Instead of attempting to control individual people from the centre, tasks and responsibilities are assigned to managers and departments. Departmental managers in turn can apply similar techniques to break their bit of the organization down to teams of one manager and a handful of people. Inside the computer this happens in the form of hierarchically organized programs of instructions, and very carefully organized information, together known as software. Only computer specialists need to be aware of these data- and information-structures.

This strategy reaches its fulfilment when we come to consider how the immense power of the computer can be made available to an ordinary user – a person who simply wishes to get things done using the computer. She neither wishes nor needs to know anything of the internal workings and representations that make her work possible. She may be a garden designer, exploring possible layouts and planting schemes. He may be a musician arranging a piece of music for the little band of players he has at his disposal. The art of the software designer is to create on the computer screen the illusion that the user (garden designer or composer) is working with ideas and concepts familiar in her or his own world of expertise. What happens between the screen and the printer is of no concern at all.

The basis for most software design (in this sense) is the human–computer interface, known universally by the acronym WIMP – Windows, Icons, Mouse and Pointer. What the user sees on the screen is a *desktop*, on which are represented *folders* containing *documents* of various kinds. Individual *applications* can be brought into play – programs that enable the user to manipulate internal representations of drawings or music.

This many-layered system relies heavily on metaphor. Each layer is described, in terms of the one below it, as a metaphor, or set of ideas and concepts, that are familiar to people working at that particular level. At the topmost level, the screen appears to be a desktop. This is simply a convenient way of enabling non-experts to use the computer employing familiar everyday ideas. In a particular window, the user sees a drawing of a garden, or a sheet of manuscript music paper. These are metaphors because they allow us to represent in familiar terms the data structures and processes at work inside the computer. By so doing, they allow users to manage extremely complex processes in order to achieve familiar goals.

In the traditional sciences, too, metaphor plays a significant part. In order to explain the phenomenon of light, physicists have resorted to metaphors of waves and particles, because under certain circumstances the behaviour of light is best explained by one metaphor (waves), while under other circumstances the other metaphor (particles) works better. Over the course of the twentieth century, research into quantum physics prompted the introduction of yet another metaphor, that of multiple parallel universes, in order to bring under one roof these diverse phenomena.[1] When developed into a mathematical model of reality, a metaphor becomes a plausible theory. Reality in itself is inaccessible; all we have to rely on is the mathematical model or metaphor.

Metaphor, then, is an idea that has planted deep roots in con-

1 See, for example, David Deutsch, *The Fabric of Reality*, London, Allen Lane, 1997.

temporary culture. One familiar idea or set of ideas is used to stand for entities in a much more complex, less readily accessible world. Of course, in the case of computer software we know that, because people made it, this complex hidden world is real. There is no doubt about its real existence. The familiar WIMP metaphors serve only to allow us to do very complex things without having to manage immense complexity.

In the world of physics, however, we may claim that the metaphor describes reality as it is, but we shall never get closer to reality than the best metaphor so far devised. For all practical purposes (at any stage of human intellectual mastery) we may argue that one metaphor serves to provide the best description of reality. But we may not claim that this is how reality *really is*. Given the fundamental principle of science, that every theory may be disproved, our current best metaphor for (or theory of) reality will probably, in time, be superseded by a better one.

In many ways ours is an uncertain age, yet people demand certainty in places where it is simply not available. Will this treatment save (or protect) my child's life? Is it safe to have this mobile phone base-station close to my home? Can you guarantee that this investment plan will give me a comfortable retirement income? Is nuclear power-generation safe? The realistic answer to all these questions is likely, at best, to be much closer to 'probably' than to 'absolutely.'

This may be a generational phenomenon. The post-war generation – the Baby-Boomers (born 1946–64) – famously 'never had it so good' (a key phrase from a speech of Prime Minister Harold Macmillan), with lifelong and assured careers during which most people found no need to change their occupation or even their employer. Successive generations have been labelled as Generation X (born 1965–79) and Generation Y (born 1980–84). Different characteristics are being found in these groups,[2] with a sense that the world's commitment to them, and their commitment to the world, are both declining.

---

2 My source here is a web page: http://blog.sironaconsulting.com/sironasays/2007/12/our-futurex-ver.html. Though it is based on what purports to be serious research, it is rather impressionistic. This doesn't mean it is wrong, merely that it needs to be taken as a clue rather than as incontrovertible proof.

It could be that this demand for certainty in certain aspects of life is a consequence of a growing sense of more general uncertainty. In a world that has reached its saturation point with regard to uncertainty, anyone who argues that the correct answer to a question should be an emphatic 'No' (or 'Yes') is likely to be heard with acclaim. Many people look to science for certainty, yet will not accept the statement of cautious probabilities with which a responsible scientist may answer their questions. In the same way, bizarrely, some look to religion for copper-bottomed assurance about the meaning of life. It would be good if religion and science were both more determined to be honest about the extent to which their positions reflect probability, belief and uncertainty.

Before we go on, there is need for a word of caution. Even precise, absolute language is subject to changes of meaning. Alexander Pope famously praised Sir Christopher Wren for his magnificent new cathedral (St Paul's) in London, describing it as 'amusing, aweful and artificial'. Each of these words has undergone a huge change of meaning in the centuries since Pope offered that compliment.

If direct language is subject to change, so too is the language of metaphor. A metaphor that works well in one culture will not necessarily cut the mustard in another. (You may have noticed an example right there. What on earth a Chinese person would make of 'cut the mustard' I have no idea!) In extolling the virtues of the metaphor we must acknowledge that many metaphors will need to be recast every time they move to a different culture. Furthermore, since the culture of a national group is not necessarily constant over an extended period of time, we must expect metaphoric usages to change as time goes by.

Metaphor in theology

Ours is an age that is almost obsessed by questions such as, 'Did it really happen like that?' Our attention is closely focused on the kind of information we might have had access to if there had been a battery of CCTV cameras around the tomb of Jesus. A Roman Catholic teacher of theology, a man with vast experience teaching in many countries, responded to a question like that by remarking that it is a quintessentially Western way of thinking. In most parts of the world, the question uppermost in students' minds would have been, 'What does it mean?'

In theology, metaphor is used to handle ideas and concepts whose existence and reality we cannot prove, and perhaps to unpack the meaning of stories. Let's go back for a moment to the garden designer using a computer to plan a planting scheme. Can we draw a parallel of any kind with the world of religious belief? Think of the business of living – getting up in the morning, choosing what to wear, dealing with relationships that aren't going well, keeping the house tidy, cooking a meal, doing a day's work, raising the children. Such a complex range of activities also involves metaphors, mental pictures that make it possible for us to navigate the day safely and successfully. We can think of the successfully managed day as the beautiful garden in the mind of the designer, our belief-system (or, for religious believers, our theology) as the set of metaphors that allows us to solve problems such as persuading teenagers to get up in the morning, or relate to their siblings less aggressively. A scientific explanation of teenage tantrums may reassure us that this is a well-known phenomenon, but it doesn't necessarily solve the problem, or calm the hurly-burly of the evening meal.

A belief-system is a set of metaphors that enables us to make sense of the lives we live as individuals, as families, as tribes, communities, nations, ethnic groups and so on. Between metaphor as used in theology and metaphor as used in, say, computing, there is a clear distinction. In our use of computers we could, if we were clever enough, understand what lies behind the metaphors that cross our computer screen. We choose not to bother because we don't need to, but in principle we could – and somebody certainly does understand (we hope). In theology, on the other hand, we use metaphor to try to describe the indescribable. In our little digression into mystery, above, we began to explore this territory. There are topics about which we can formulate ideas and undergo experiences, yet which are not amenable to description except by the use of metaphor.

One cluster of uses of metaphor is linked to the idea of time. Time can serve as a metaphor to help us understand other ideas, but in itself it is sufficient of a puzzle that we use other metaphors to describe time itself. Think, for example, of the use in film of time-lapse photography to suggest the passage of time in a narrative: clouds move swiftly across the scene, the alternation of day and night becomes a flicker; we know that time has passed.

The use of time as a metaphor is of course not limited to theology. Think of 'the river of time' as a way of expressing the way time flows always and only in the same direction. It is one of the most perplexing of life's puzzles. Why does it flow only in one direction? Why can we not retrace our steps? What is it that connects the person you are today with the person who went unwillingly to school many years ago? What has time done to you?

When we say of someone that 'she always likes to have the last word', what exactly are we saying? The last word is the one that marks the end of debate, the time for decision. The last word is often the one that sticks in the memory for the longest time. The last word is the one that cannot be refuted because all opportunity for refutation is over; the point at issue is decided. It may be that the insistence on saying the last word is a way of rejecting the conversation partner's ideas, and perhaps the conversation partner himself (or herself).

There are of course people who treat this as a game. Having the last word is simply a ploy to ensure that they have in some sense won the game, though it is often so obvious what is going on that others make appropriate allowances and ignore what they've said!

In the Bible, time is important. Genesis 1 is often viewed as the earliest creation story in the Bible, simply because it appears to address questions about the beginning of time and we find it on page 1. In fact, it probably isn't the earliest such story (other cultures had their own such stories too[3]), and it isn't about creation – at least, not in the modern scientific sense. It has much in common with other creation stories from around the world (though which is the original and which are derivative is a very tangled question). From ancient legends, it assumed its present form at the head of a body of literature designed to explain to the

3 See, for example, Ellen J. van Wolde, *Stories of the Beginning: Genesis 1–11 and Other Creation Stories*, Harrisburg, Pennsylvania, Morehouse, 1997.

people of Judaea their own origins as a people and their place in the created order.[4] In this account, *order* is a key concept, implying not merely a sequence of creation but a whole network of proper, orderly relationships, ranging from mixing different types of cloth in a garment to the importance of observing the distinction between one day (the Sabbath) and other days. Any violation of these relationships will damage the integrity of the community and their central relationship – with God, who first established these proper orderings. The thrust of these stories of creation is that order is not merely man-made, arbitrary or conventional. From this can be deduced (among other things) a system of ethical rules to guide us in our relationships with one another. Now, it has to be admitted that this position – of absolute ethical rules handed down from on high – is contentious. Many have argued that there is a rational basis for all ethical decisions, and if no rational defence can be found, then those ethical judgements must be questioned. So 'There is' mutates almost imperceptibly into 'There must be'.

At the other end of the Bible we see the same phenomenon: things of ultimate importance are presented in the form of stories and pictures about the end of time.

And 'now', the present moment, has its own particular significance for biblical culture. Now is the day of salvation! The present moment is the moment for us to make choices!

There are jokes about human choice, like the story of the visitor to America who goes into a fast-food restaurant and orders a coffee. To his great surprise he is immediately offered a bewildering abundance of choice: where the beans come from, how the beans were prepared, how the coffee is served, with milk or cream, chocolate grounds on top, whisky mixed in – you name it. While he's making his decision, the people in the queue behind him become irritated, he becomes increasingly bemused and

---

4 This argument is set out in a fascinating but (it has to be said) controversial book by Richard Elliott Friedman, *Who Wrote the Bible?*, Englewood Cliffs, New Jersey, Prentice Hall, 1987. Friedman argues that although the 'creation stories' of Genesis 1 and 2 have deep roots in Israel's prehistory, the compilation of the Old Testament as we know it probably took place around the period of the Exile, in part as a way to place on record their origins as a people.

eventually leaves with no coffee at all. But a Christian reading of life (which we sometimes refer to as God's great project) rests precisely on our freedom to choose.

Time, then, is a metaphor in itself. But, like many metaphors, it is culturally determined. Anyone who has been a guest or officiant at an African wedding or funeral will understand that in some other cultures time has a very different meaning compared with Western, clock-driven time. Religions of the Far East, such as Buddhism, operate within a framework in which time is circular; this life, through reincarnation, may be lived many times, though in different guises. The Abrahamic faiths – Judaism, Christianity and Islam – work with a linear model of time: there is a beginning, a middle, and an end, not only for our individual lives, but for time itself. It is hardly surprising, then, that the uses to which the metaphor of time is put will vary according to cultural context. Its explanatory power in one culture will probably not be matched in another.

We shall find this idea – the centrality of time – playing a large part in our discussion of Jesus.

Mythos and *logos*

A myth is a story whose elements (agents and events) are not read as literally true, but are instead read as corresponding to some supernatural or transnatural realm which in turn is related intuitively, rather than factually, to the real world. These elements are metaphors for real entities or events. The important feature of myth is that it tells a story with which people caught up in the toils of everyday life at its most mysterious and impenetrable can identify.[5]

An excellent introduction to the notion of myth in religious and scientific usage can be found in Ian Barbour's book *Myths,*

5 A good account can be found in the article by J. W. Rogerson, 'Myth', in Richard James Coggins and James Leslie Houlden (eds), *A Dictionary of Biblical Interpretation*, London, SCM Press and Philadelphia, Trinity Press International, 1990.

Models and Paradigms.[6] Barbour went on to write two further major books, *Religion in an Age of Science*, and *Ethics in an Age of Technology*. Here, however, he structured a classification of the uses of symbolic language. Describing post-war trends in philosophy, he points out that the age of logical positivism – in which only those statements could be admitted as meaningful which correspond to observable reality – is past; there are many ways in which language is used to convey meaning, not all of them tied to objective phenomena.

> Myths are stories which are taken to manifest some aspect of the cosmic order. They provide a community with ways of interpreting experience in the present. They inform man about his self-identity and the framework of significance in which he participates . . . Myths are re-enacted in rituals which integrate the community around common memories and common goals.[7]

Again Barbour offers a number of ways in which myths serve humanity: myths offer ways of ordering experience; they inform humans about themselves; they express a saving power in human life; they provide patterns for human action; they are enacted in rituals.

Barbour proposes the notion of a *model* which is embodied in a myth or a coherent series of myths. A creation myth may be no more than a way of grappling with the intractable questions about 'how all this stuff came to be'. But coupled with other stories such as death and resurrection, it suggests a model which can provide fertile ground for addressing unforeseen situations. A *paradigm* is a larger, more comprehensive system of knowledge and procedure which guides practitioners in the way they conduct investigations, handle debates, evaluate evidence and so on.

I have concluded that it would be good to extend the treatment of metaphor to include the categories of myth and allegory. This may help strengthen in readers' minds the idea that the Church

6 Ian G. Barbour, *Myths, Models and Paradigms: The Nature of Scientific and Religious Language*, San Francisco, Harper & Row, 1974.

7 Barbour, *Myths, Models and Paradigms*, pp. 20ff.

has read the Bible in many different ways over the course of the Christian centuries; the present notion of biblical literalism is a recent development, probably in response to Enlightenment assaults on the credibility of the Bible as factual scientific history. It is important that the integrity of the Bible be respected. But modern readers may be very surprised to learn something of the techniques of biblical interpretation that have been favoured over the centuries. Many of these are startlingly at variance with anything we might recognize in popular literature about the Bible today. In particular, they bear no relation to the insistence on biblical literalism so favoured by Christian conservatives, which is in fact a twentieth-century development.

Indeed the whole idea of biblical interpretation is anathema to such conservative thinkers. In an article by Harriet Harris on fundamentalism in *The Oxford Handbook of Biblical Studies*,[8] the creation scientist David C. C. Watson is quoted thus: 'Scripture requires no more interpretation than do the cricket scores in your morning paper.'

The category of myth fell into disuse in biblical scholarship following scornful dismissal by the rationalist advocates of a scientific worldview. So, it has been almost a working principle in such circles that the Bible contains no myths as such: what you read is what you get; what you read is what is. Nevertheless, even this very rigorous position does not exclude altogether the possibility that the biblical stories can benefit from being read as myths, almost without regard to their historicity. The mythic meaning may be true, regardless of whether the story is factually true or not.

Another category of biblical interpretation much favoured in the Middle Ages is that of the *type*. A *type* is a pattern set out in one story (or series of stories) which is followed by another story; the second story is then interpreted in terms of the first. Thus the figure of Moses as leader and deliverer is a *type* of Christ, the leader and deliverer. Such models of biblical interpretation encouraged scholars to reflect on the character of Moses' story as providing insight into the story of Jesus.

---

8 J. W. Rogerson and J. Lieu, *The Oxford Handbook of Biblical Studies*, Oxford, Oxford University Press, 2006, p. 817.

On the basis of this very brief discussion we make two observations.

First, the use of myth, allegory and type – and other such non-literal schemes of interpretation – in biblical scholarship is not directly connected with the factuality or otherwise of the biblical story. To grasp the story of Exodus or Exile (two formative biblical events) as mythic does not imply any judgement at all about whether or not they actually happened in the way the Bible appears to claim they did.

Second, the use of allegory and type has been found helpful to Christians in various ways throughout history. They have fallen out of fashion and have been restored to favour. For various reasons, the category of myth has fallen out of favour as a scholarly tool in handling ancient Christian texts. But Christian believing is not primarily about whether a particular interpretive tool is in fashion or out of fashion, or even about whether the story itself is 'true' in a narrow scientific–historical sense; it is about appropriating the story, identifying our own life and the life of our community with the biblical narrative, letting the story help us navigate and negotiate our way through life, receiving the insight and awareness that is exposed as we approach the story in an indirect way.

In his book *Myth, History and Faith*[9] Morton Kelsey discusses the changes that have taken place over the centuries with respect to the place of myth in the context of faith. Kelsey points to the influence of Aristotle, notably through the work of St Thomas Aquinas. I can explain this best in relation to the categories of *mythos* and *logos* deployed so effectively by Karen Armstrong in her book *The Battle for God*.[10] As a rough guide, *mythos* reflects a worldview that seeks meaning in stories – stories which, to use the memorable phrase of Kierkegaard, reflect 'the way things never were but always are'. Some myths are clearly fictions, invented for the specific purpose of bearing a meaning that can be expressed in no other way. Other myths begin as legends or plausibly true

9 M. T. Kelsey, *Myth, History and Faith: The Remythologizing of Christianity*, New York, Paulist Press, 1974.

10 K. Armstrong, *The Battle for God*, London, HarperCollins, 2000, p. xiii and many other references.

stories but assume mythic status through long familiarity, adaptation and use. Myth, then, is more about the way we use a story than it is about the story itself. In our use of myth the important element is the way an individual or a community can identify with the elements of the story and so overcome the deep personal challenges of living, making sacrifices, enduring hardship, and dying. Its influence can thus be hugely beneficial, but it can also be catastrophic, as when the Norse myths were deployed to enable the German people to recover their sense of identity and self-esteem after the humiliation of defeat in the First World War.

Logos, on the other hand, seeks meaning in fact and reason. It is the basis of scientific investigation, and of the technological re-fashioning of the world. Given the astonishing achievements of *logos*, it is not really surprising that its practitioners should doubt the value of any other worldview.

Kelsey[11] describes the pattern of understanding the world that prevailed before the eleventh century, when Aristotelian thinking reached Western Europe (through the influence, among others, of Arab scholars). Following the teachings of Plato, the other giant of Ancient Greece alongside Aristotle, there were understood to be three ways of knowing:

1 Sense experience.
2 Reason.
3 Direct contact with non-physical reality (Plato called this 'divine madness'), or revelation.

Myths were a result of this last kind of knowing. (Of course, our atheist contemporaries would deny that talk of 'non-physical reality' has any meaning at all.)

The optimal mix of sense experience and reason had yet to emerge, but as that optimal mix evolved over the following centuries it hugely enhanced the power of science to provide explanations for real-world phenomena. Alongside this, science gained in power to command our view of the world.

As a consequence of the rise in Aristotelian thinking, the *logos*

11 Kelsey, *Myth, History and Faith*.

pattern of thought has dominated Catholic and Protestant theology ever since Aquinas. In Catholicism, however, the mythic element has been powerfully sustained in the liturgy, leaving Protestant denominations in the grip of *logos*.

In the twentieth century, however, a succession of global calamities – notably two world wars – sapped confidence both in pure rationality and in myth. The twentieth-century work of Rudolf Bultmann (and his followers like John Robinson in his controversial book *Honest to God*[12]) in attempting to discard the element of *mythos* in Christianity, is a reversion to the dazzling logic of St Thomas and through him to Aristotle. The project to demythologize Christianity began not with Bultmann but with Aquinas, and Aquinas' thinking rested in turn on his rediscovery of the work of Aristotle.

Kelsey's little book goes on to argue that, so far from banishing *mythos* from Christianity, it is absolutely vital that we should rehabilitate *mythos* within Christianity, and value it, alongside *logos*, *chaos*, and uncertainty, as an essential component of our knowing, believing, trusting and practice. Indeed, we can go further: the wholeness, the *shalom*, of the world community, will be found in balance between these aspects in all human life. They are not opposed to one another; none need be demonized.

Kelsey's argument is that *mythos* is in fact an indispensable element in our humanity. He points to a number of instances in which distressed people are healed through the experience of identification with a myth. In Kelsey's view, the role of religion is to provide us with tools to engage with myth in a positive manner.

A change has taken place not only in the status of myth as a concept, but also in the use of the word 'myth' to mean *a lie*. Can we rehabilitate the word 'myth'? I think I may have a possible answer, in the word 'symbolic'. Take a word like 'donkey'. It denotes a particular kind of domesticated animal. The word 'donkey' can therefore be seen as a symbol directly representing such an animal. We may call this first-order symbolism. In that sense, all language exhibits first-order symbolism, so the word 'symbolic' appears unable to help us. But if we use 'donkey' metaphorically,

12 J. A. T. Robinson, *Honest to God*, London, SCM Press, 1963, pp. 143.

to mean a stupid or obstinate person, then the word 'donkey' is symbolic in two senses: first, it denotes the domestic animal, and then (perhaps through the well-known attributes of that animal) it stands for something else. The word 'donkey', then, stands not for the actual animal, but for an attribute of the animal which can then be transferred to something (or someone) else. It is in this second-order sense that I want to use the word 'symbolic'.

In this sense, 'symbolic' can be used of words and the associations they evoke (as in the case of the donkey); it can also be used of stories which, though not factual (i.e. they don't represent or stand for actual events, so they aren't first-order symbols) nevertheless convey meaning. So a myth is a symbolic story.

There is, of course, no obstacle to a real story being also a symbolic story, just as there is no difficulty in the use of the word 'donkey' as a first-order and a second-order symbol.

There is another word which I think has a bearing on this notion of symbolic language. It is the word 'abstraction', as used in mathematics. Many of us have struggled with problems in applied mathematics at school in which we considered the motion of a ball rolling down an inclined plane. When we consider such motion, there are properties of the ball and the plane that we can ignore – for example, whether they are made of wood or steel, whether they are painted blue or green; and there are properties that are, or may be, essential to our calculation – are they smooth or rough, hard or soft. It is common practice in mathematics to use this principle of abstraction to strip away from a real-world problem everything that does not play a part in formulating the problem as a mathematical one and therefore making it amenable to a mathematical solution. Subsequently the principle of abstraction has found application in the realm of computer software design.

Is there a relationship between abstraction and symbolic language?

In working with our metaphorical donkey, what seems to be happening is this. Here is a donkey with an exceedingly large number of attributes: age, height, weight, number of hairs on its body, and so on. In its behaviour it may be stubborn, tractable, docile, unpredictable or bad-tempered. There is, however, a stereotypical view of a donkey which singles out its stupidity and stubbornness as wholly characteristic of the species. This characteristic is then abstracted from the far more complex picture of a real donkey, and used as the basis of a metaphor. That's what we mean when we describe someone as 'Such a donkey!'

Most stories are quite evidently abstractions. They do not describe in full the events of a day or a week in the lives of the principal characters. Through most ordinary lives run a number of threads; most novels are limited to one or perhaps two. Leading figures in thrillers never have routine hospital appointments, elderly relatives never phone to report a family bereavement, personal relationships outside the storyline are only ever incidental, and often carry uncomfortable baggage. This drives the hero into the closed and manageable circle of people involved in the investigation, whether as fellow-investigators, witnesses or suspects. Where such distractions are mentioned, they often appear to have been contrived as a way of balancing the narrow focus of the storyline with the demand that it must be recognizably connected with real life.

Right at the beginning of the Bible, the book of Genesis tells of the origins of a particular people. The story is narrated through the characters of a few individuals – patriarchs. In these men – and their wives play a profoundly significant role too – we are invited to see the human condition in all its sordid glory. Their ventures in faith, not to mention their blunders, are examined with great insight. Behind these stories of individuals, entire families and tribes move in the shadows. It is a wonderful example of abstraction.

2

Religion in the Modern World

The language of Zion

In Chapter 1 we saw that there is a great variety in the ways in which we use language. Sometimes we are at pains to use language in the most direct way. This would be appropriate if, for example, we were writing instructions on how to assemble an item of flat-packed furniture, or how to use public transport to reach a particular destination. But there are other ways of using language – metaphor, myth and so on – which we call upon when our subject matter is not amenable to such *plain meaning* patterns of use.

In former times, our Christian forefathers might have referred to 'the language of Zion', in which the distinctive elements of Christian linguistic usage seem very strange and obscure – even repellent[1] – to the modern reader. While such language is less fashionable now, even within church circles, there remains a reverent attachment to the traditional language of Christian theology, an attachment which can be stubborn – and perhaps unthinking.

In prayers, hymns, worship and conversation, Christians still use a language that seems strange and unfamiliar to anyone who is not a regular churchgoer – simply because it sounds antiquated and its claims verge on the absurd. Moreover, because it is not the language of every day, it is difficult to engage with and hard to question. In an age characterized by a freedom to question, that creates impenetrable barriers for many people.

This unfamiliarity arises for two reasons. First, Christians use a vocabulary in which words have a technical meaning. I'm talking

1 'Washed in the blood of the lamb' is a case in point.

about terms such as 'salvation', 'covenant', 'virgin birth', 'resurrection', God, the Holy Spirit, and so on. Christian people may or may not be deeply familiar with the technical usage of these words, but they use them nonetheless, and such Christians can sometimes look suspiciously on folk who ask them what exactly they mean by these terms. The second reason is that the way in which the Christian faith is very often expressed relies very heavily on the patterns of indirect reference that we introduced in Chapter 1.

Part of the problem is this. Because its subject matter is not the everyday stuff of bus journeys, business contracts, sports reports, benefit claim forms and so on, Christian speech and writing relies heavily on those devices of indirect reference like metaphor. Yet Christian communicators often insist, nevertheless, that what they say is on a par with that everyday stuff: it deals with 'real things'. An example is that, thanks to the way in which it is set out, the Creed appears to provide a series of final, conclusive answers. In the first instance, of course, this is exactly what they were designed to do. But today we may prefer to see theology as an ongoing journey of exploration – a continuing 'work in progress'. The language is so technical and antique, however, that its true character, as a work in progress rather than a final solution, is often overlooked. The technical specialists seem sometimes to collude with this concealment; it provides them with a mystique, an expertise, which further distances 'God talk' from the world in which ordinary people live. There is, too, for many pastors and preachers, a genuine concern for those who have no appetite for inquiry and debate, and would find it a grave challenge to their faith.

Four responses

To the use of such language there are at least four possible responses:

1 There are no real concepts to which the words refer. All such usage is akin to fairy-tales. Their continued circulation is positively harmful.

2 These words do indeed refer to real concepts, events and entities, and the only satisfactory way to work with them is to take them literally, 'at face value'.
3 These words do indeed correspond to real concepts, events and entities, but the best way to look at them is as metaphors.
4 Coming full circle, there are no real concepts to which the words refer (as in 1 above), but their usage is legitimate because it provides people with something to hang on to. It legitimates activities, like rituals, that people value and find helpful.

Of these four, options 2 and 3 fall squarely within the spectrum of religious belief. Options 1 (certainly) and 4 (possibly) would be regarded by most people as falling outside that category. There is, however, a worthwhile distinction between options 1 and 4. Although they each claim that the words mean nothing, option 1 points chiefly to the harmful effects of religion and concludes that on balance the world would be better off without it. Option 4, on the other hand, recognizes that, for all committed believers and most half-believers, religious belief serves a worthwhile purpose.

In recent years the first option has been propagated very aggressively by distinguished writers such as Richard Dawkins,[2] Christopher Hitchens[3] and Daniel Dennett.[4] Religious language, they say, is devoid of meaning; it refers to nothing, and its use adds nothing to our understanding of anything. Far from being neutral, moreover, religion is positively harmful. Many wicked and violent things have been done on the basis of a particular understanding of what religious language means; to train the young (or indeed anyone) to believe what is manifestly contrary to the evidence of reason and the senses is to stunt and warp their development. From these two propositions – religious language is meaningless, and its use is harmful – these writers argue with no little passion that the world would be a better place without it. I believe that, where what they say is correct, the religious world would do well to pay attention, even if it makes us feel very uncom-

2 R. Dawkins, *The God Delusion*, London, Bantam Press, 2006.

3 C. Hitchens, *God is Not Great: How Religion Poisons Everything*, New York, Twelve, 2007.

4 D. C. Dennett, *Breaking the Spell*, London, Allen Lane, 2006.

fortable. Lofty dismissal is not an appropriate response. Several writers have tried to respond to this onslaught.[5] These writers are in general remarkable for their scholarly rigour, forbearance and courtesy in the face of the vituperative scorn of those whom Beattie calls 'The New Atheists'.

The influence of the second alternative appears to be rising rapidly in the world's communities of faith.[6] It is popular for a number of reasons, not the least of which is its offer of attractive certainties in the face of uneasy ambiguity. One name for it is fundamentalism. A characteristic surface feature is the rejection of each and every way of understanding religious language and ideas apart from a simple, direct and literal one – this is option 1 above. Thus, people who think like this *tend* to cast a suspicious eye on those whose position is closer to alternative three. 'You're not a *real* Christian', or perhaps 'You're not a *real* Muslim.' Incidentally, I chose the word 'tend' with care, to avoid suggesting that *everyone* who thinks like this will be dismissive of people who don't think as they do.

More deeply significant is the rejection of modernism, a system of knowledge and truth-claims based on rational inquiry, particularly where such knowledge and truth-claims are in conflict with religious revelation or, more narrowly, with a specific *interpretation* of revelation. Examples of such 'revealed knowledge' include the claims that the world was created in six 24-hour days, some 6,000 years ago, and that homosexuality is an abhorrent deviation, deserving of no recognition or acceptance. Both the claims are in conflict with modernist views that claim to be based on objective observation.

In the third alternative, religious language is largely, perhaps entirely, *metaphorical*. That is, its words *do* refer to real entities, events and concepts, but *not* '*literally*'; rather, the reference

5 See, for example, K. Ward, *Is Religion Dangerous?*, Oxford, Lion, 2006; A. E. McGrath and J. McGrath, *The Dawkins Delusion: Atheist Fundamentalism and the Denial of the Divine*, Downers Grove, Illinois, InterVarsity Press, 2007; and T. Beattie, *The New Atheists: The Twilight of Reason and the War on Religion*, Maryknoll, New York, Orbis Books, 2008.

6 This has been catalogued admirably in K. Armstrong, *The Battle for God*, London, HarperCollins, 2000.

is oblique, allusive or poetic. (This is discussed more fully in the next chapter.) This indirectness does not mean that the notions referred to are unreal, fantastic or unimportant, or that the statements made are devoid of content. Rather, it is a statement about the capacity of language to express ideas. Empirical 'scientific' language, for example, lacks the expressive power to structure and work with these notions in a manner that meets the needs of the human heart. A scientist may one day be able to describe the physiological and biochemical changes in my body when I listen to the music of Mozart or Mahler. His description may well be faultless and complete, in the sense that it embraces fully and perfectly every aspect of the matter that science is able to address. But his words will add nothing to my enjoyment of the music, nor will they work, for me, as an explanation of why I find that music so profoundly supportive of my humanity.[7]

The fourth alternative is, approximately, that held by the non-realist writer Don Cupitt. To borrow the title of one of his books,[8] he has 'taken leave of God'. His ideas have been taken up by a group calling themselves the 'Sea of Faith' movement, following the poem 'On Dover Beach', by Matthew Arnold. In many ways this view is very close to option 1, and to many – believers and non-believers alike – the two are indistinguishable. They both speak in terms of a category of meaningless statements, following the line developed by the philosopher A. J. Ayer. So, we may say, there is a categoric equivalence between them. But advocates of option 1 would insist that for an individual or a community to adopt and base their existence on the truth of meaningless statements is nothing but folly – and dangerous folly at that, because not only is there no way of proving their claims true, there is no way, either, of proving them false. Cupitt, on the other hand, would want to admit (insofar as I understand him) that to follow

7 I have been reminded that this statement about the music of Mozart and Mahler is a highly personal one. Others will not find that classical music 'does it' for them. For others, music of a different kind does, while some people simply do not respond to music at all. While I may long to share with them what it is that I get out of my kind of music, I hesitate to offer value judgements about their preferences.

8 D. Cupitt, *Taking Leave of God*, London, SCM Press, 1980.

such a system of belief can bring benefits that other belief-systems cannot bring. So, between them (options 1 and 4), there is an *economic* distinction; while their nature may be very similar, they function in quite different ways.

I have long felt that the first two options present us with a false dichotomy; the choice between them does not cover all the ground. The fourth I regard as, to all intents and purposes, equivalent to the first – though Cupitt is much less given to dismissive and vitriolic scorn. It is to the third, therefore, that I turn in my attempt to understand better both my own faith and the faith of the Church.

Though in the general population all four patterns will be found, readers who have come with me this far may well have reached very similar conclusions to my own with no great fuss. You may wonder why I am making such a song and dance about it. It is, surely, all so very obvious. I have two responses to this concern.

The first is one of alarm at the false dichotomy I referred to above, the degree to which conversation on this subject is polarized between those who take position 1 – the 'meaningless fairy-tales' position – and those who take position 2 – who, for want of a better word, we may refer to as the fundamentalists, while acknowledging that we need to be rather careful about the way we use that word. Debate is turning into a shouting match between groups who not only do not understand each other, but who refuse to admit even the *possibility* of understanding each other. Dawkins, for example, appears to *define* the term 'Christian' according to his rather selective impression of the most extreme and most irrational among believers. Any Christian who does not fit this extreme definition he is liable to dismiss as not a real Christian at all! And on the 'believers' side, there is a strong tendency for some to view their 'take' on religion as not merely *closer to* the truth than others but actually to *be* the truth. While dialogues of the deaf rage between radical atheists and believers, so they rage also between one sort of believer and another.

I find each of these alternatives equally oppressive and equally inadequate. Each 'side' seems intent on setting up its opponents as despicable caricatures, to the extent that the discussion has long since lost any real value. On each side protagonists are praying (in their own way) for the extinction of the other – not personally, of course, but in terms of the ideas they represent.

I would like to think that those who find option 3 preferable would nonetheless extend a degree of respect to positions 1, 2 and 4, at least in the sense that all three of these options belong (together with option 3) to a community of disagreement in which each can stimulate the others to sharper and more self-aware thinking. My difficulty with them is that the advocates of positions 1, 2 and 4 seem unwilling to offer a reciprocal welcome.

So, my second, and deeper, response is grounded in a concern that a form of reasoned religious modernism survives the crossfire of this, increasingly meaningless, battle. A world in which either of these ideologies (1 and 2) held absolute sway (which seems to be what each demands) would be intolerable. There must be an alternative place in which people of wisdom can find a home.

That is the attraction of alternative 3, although it could be argued that this view represents an unwillingness to commit to the teachings of the Church. While this may indeed seem to be the case, it is nonetheless a valid position on a lifetime's journey struggling with these ideas. As we have argued above, theology is a work in progress. Günther Weber[9] has set out a strong case for doubt as the essential companion for belief.

Perhaps, too, it needs to be admitted that part of faith is the possibility of being found wrong, that the attraction of alternative 3, to which I referred above, might be illusory – wishful thinking even. However much St Paul may have been persuaded of the saving power of Jesus Christ, it is possible that his hope may be an empty one and that Christians may (in the end) be, of all people, the most to be pitied (to quote St Paul again).[10] An inquiring faith is, at some level, an uncertain faith. At its heart it is confident, but there is within it an urgent pulse of inquiry as to the shape and meaning of what is believed.

There are three classic creeds of the Western Church: the Apostles' Creed, the Nicene Creed and the Athanasian Creed.

9 G. N. Weber, *I Believe, I Doubt: Notes on Christian Experience*, London, SCM Press, 1998.

10 1 Corinthians 15.12–19 (New Revised Standard Version).

Each was born out of its historical context, but Christians use them – and some are confused by them – quite independently of the strenuous logic that brought them to birth. The Apostles' Creed forms the basis for the second part of this book on the Content of Believing, but it would be unfortunate if this book were to be read as a new study of the Apostles' Creed as a historical document setting out the content of faith. Always the aim will be to try to 'get behind' the words to see what they might mean.

It is that 'urgent pulse' that has driven me to write this book. In following that urgent pulse I stand in a very long and eminent tradition. Here is a brief quotation from the Stanford Encyclopaedia of Philosophy.[11] It refers to Anselm (*c.* 1033–1109), Archbishop of Canterbury in the eleventh century.

> Anselm's motto is 'faith seeking understanding' (*fides quaerens intellectum*). This motto lends itself to at least two misunderstandings. First, many philosophers have taken it to mean that Anselm hopes to replace faith with understanding. If one takes 'faith' to mean roughly 'belief on the basis of testimony' and 'understanding' to mean 'belief on the basis of philosophical insight', one is likely to regard faith as an epistemically substandard position; any self-respecting philosopher would surely want to leave faith behind as quickly as possible.

Indeed, this slogan can reasonably be described as the thrust behind all Christian theology. As pointed out by another writer on Anselm, however, Anselm's aim was not to replace faith with understanding. For Anselm, faith is a love for God and a drive to act as God wills. In this, Anselm's position was echoed seven centuries later by John Wesley, who declared that 'faith is not a train of ideas in the head; it is a disposition of the heart'.

What, then, in the mind of the theologian, is the relationship between love and understanding? At heart they are mutually informative; the love for God provides the 'urgent pulse of inquiry', while the hard thinking and reflecting – the seeking – connects faith with the rest of human life, so enabling the believer to give

11 The text can be found at http://plato.stanford.edu/entries/anselm/.

an account of the faith that is within him. Any reader who is troubled by the thought of deconstructing or tampering with the classic declarations of faith of the Church can set her fears on one side. Each human generation of Christians faces the same problem: how to take this language and these thought-forms, which undoubtedly took shape in the ancient world, and interpret them for and make them intelligible to the contemporary world. In this we have various sources of information: the classic creeds (one of which provides the framework for a major part of this book); the ways in which previous generations have addressed this problem for their own age; and our knowledge of the world around us.

There is a corollary to this. When we have (at least provisionally) satisfied our desire for new expressions of faith, we may – indeed we must – share them with our own and succeeding generations. What we may not do is to substitute them for the classic creeds. We are not entitled to say to future generations, 'New readers start here' using our new expressions of faith as their starting-point.

That, however, is not the end of our journey, for it will take us a little to one side in its emphasis on the content of belief – on the propositions we are asked, as Christians, to hold to be true. Our goal is to understand a little better what it means to be a Christian, and how 'believing' works as a part of that bigger picture.

Postmodernism

Over the course of the last millennium the patterns of human thought have undergone several momentous changes.

In the pre-modern Christian world (roughly before about 1200 CE) the only channel through which humanity acquired knowledge (other than immediately practical knowledge) was that of revelation.[12] In the terms of this book, the transcendent mysteriously chose to disclose itself (or not). Since the transcendent is beyond the reach of human rational investigation, revealed truth

12 The beginnings of scientific inquiry lie, of course, long before this date, in Greek, Egyptian, Babylonian, Persian and Chinese cultures. The account given here focuses specifically on the story of Christian civilization.

is beyond dispute. The over-arching story, the 'big picture', is revelation.

Over the next five or six centuries the modern view of things rose to prominence. On this view, everything is subject to rational inquiry; no question is inherently off-limits. The only mechanism for the acquisition of knowledge is that involving observation and reason; revelation has no place whatsoever. The over-arching story here is the application of reason. Like revelation before it, this observation-plus-reason view lays claim to universal validity and acceptance. Essential to it is the notion of objectivity: what one person sees, others can see too, under the same reproducible circumstances. This philosophy led to a kind of optimism, that by the application of reason the human world could solve all its problems and overcome all its ills.

With the rise of global warfare in the twentieth century, this optimism faded, and with it any notion of a universal over-arching story. As we have seen, over the same time period science experienced a somewhat chastening series of changes in the realm of modern physics. The 'grand narrative' of revelation has failed; the grand narrative of empirical reason has clearly not solved all human problems.[13] A view has taken hold in the bleached desert of these past failures, which is known as *postmodernism*.[14] As a result, I do not have a privileged position from which to tell you what to believe – and nor does anyone else. In the popular mind this has led to the rejection of authority, the cultivation of the view that 'my opinion is as good as anyone else's', and the phenomenon of 'commitment phobia'. No cause can any

---

13 At the Labour Party Conference, on 25 October 2007, the Foreign Secretary David Miliband reviewed the lessons learned from the attempt by the West to establish a democratic order in Iraq and Afghanistan. He said that while there may be military *victories*, there can never be a military *solution*. Perhaps the same could be said of empirical reason: it can provide solutions to some problems, but it cannot pretend to offer an all-embracing description of things.

14 A useful introduction to these ideas, from a Christian perspective, can be found in a book by Stanley J. Grenz, *A Primer on Postmodernism*, Grand Rapids, Michigan; Cambridge, William B. Eerdmans, 1996. Terry Eagleton has written a very searching critique of the postmodernism fashion: T. Eagleton, *The Illusions of Postmodernism*, Oxford, Blackwell Publishers, 1996.

longer recruit widespread and active engagement. One philosopher, Francis Fukuyama, has even written of 'the end of history'[15] – though he later retracted this.

We have now entered the world of postmodernism. The characteristic feature of this period is the claim that there is no universally acceptable account of how things are, how things came to be, who we are, where are we going, what life is all about. Neither revelation nor reason can give us the answers we are looking for. In fact, nothing outside of ourselves can give us answers. The only answers are those we create for ourselves.

We can see this in the widespread rejection of scientific and engineering arguments about the risks involved in vaccination, genetically modified foods and mobile telephones. Science is no longer the source of a trusted set of common values.

There is a widespread misconception that science is about certainty. It is not. On the contrary, it is about provisional knowledge that is always subject to challenge and correction. A major task of popular expositors of science is precisely to clarify this position, to make it clear that people who are looking for absolute certainty (about, for example, the hazards arising from development in technology) are asking the impossible.

It is not only science that has lost its position of unquestioned authority. The same is true of government, and (as we have seen) religion. Why is this? Philosophically, it is because (according to postmodernism) the world is in fact our own construction. It's all in our own heads. There is no basis of agreement between us; we have to choose, each one of us, how we wish to see and understand the world.

This corresponds very closely to the world of consumer capitalism. When mass production of automobiles first began, Henry Ford could famously say, 'You can have any colour you like so long as it's black'.[16] Now we can customize our car, customize our diet, our house, our holidays, our clothes, even the shape of our bodies. Any attempt to lay down a 'collective view' or restrict free-

15 F. Fukuyama, *The End of History and the Last Man*, London, Hamish Hamilton, 1992.

16 In fact this was true only after 1914 – five years after the Model T was introduced.

dom of choice is dismissed as oppressive. During my youth it was possible to meet my schoolfriends and discuss what was broadcast the previous evening. There was, after all, only one television channel, so television provided a shared experience for everyone who had access to a television. Now, with many channels and many possible ways of receiving a signal (or, to use the modern term, 'viewing content'), everyone's experience is different.

It is surely worthy of note that voices have been raised decrying this trend towards the personalized lifestyle.

A second measure of change is the sense in which the problem of the human condition is no longer characterized simply as moral failure. The old categories of Sin and Evil, linked with notions of the sacred and ritual impurity, carry less weight than once they did, though in the public response to paedophilia and child abuse generally they are clearly not far from the surface. Traditionally (starting with St Augustine of Hippo and his interpretation of the story in Genesis 3), sin's point of entry into human life has been held to be women. The story of such misogynist bias is both horrifying and profoundly depressing. Perhaps with the growing sense of outrage against what is seen to be primarily, if not exclusively, a male betrayal of trust, the balance is shifting in the other direction!

A great theologian of the mid-twentieth century, Paul Tillich, identified this problem with a sense of *estrangement*, a feeling of not belonging.[17] Others have described it in terms of meaninglessness. A careful reading of the New Testament characterizes sin not simply as immoral conduct towards other people, but as failure to recognize and acknowledge Jesus as God's special representative. John's Gospel is explicit: failure to believe in Jesus as God's Son is at the root of all human disorientation and misery.

In general terms, then, moral failure is not the place where most people are hurting. Other ideas, such as the lack of meaning and purpose in life, the sense of not belonging, the vague and hard-to-define sense of estrangement from life – these are the hurting-places now. All too often they flare up in the form of aggressive assertions of identity, both for individuals and groups.

---

17 P. Tillich, *The Shaking of the Foundations*, Harmondsworth, Penguin, 1962, p. 185.

3

Narrating the Truth

In the previous chapter we have seen ways of reading words and word-pictures – extracting meaning from words – that do not depend upon their literal correspondence with reality. The central part of this book will rely heavily on these non-literal approaches. There remains, however, another avenue in our journey around the garden of language: story. It is impossible to talk about the Bible at all without using the word 'story', but even in this context it is often used in a way that suggests, but does not explore or develop, a much wider set of ideas. The notion of 'story' pervades this book just as much as does the word 'metaphor'. We look first to the world of science to help us develop a richer understanding of how stories are related to truth.

Stories in science

In this section I want to look at the way stories function in science. It may be that this will help us create a map or framework that will be helpful to our later thinking.

Here are two stories of scientific investigations. The first gives a general, if somewhat idealized, account of how scientific research works.

When a scientist is grappling with a problem ('Why did that happen?') her first instinct is to think of a possible mechanism that could cause it to happen – in other words, an explanation. We call this a conjecture or hypothesis – essentially a guess. (In the vast majority of cases this guess will be grounded in a great deal of experience and knowledge, so the word 'guess' shouldn't be taken as dismissive.) Occasionally, when the problem is especially baffling, the guess may be a wild one. Whether the hypothesis is wild or based on long experience, what follows will be essentially the same. Our scientist will think about the hypothesis, which took shape as a possible explanation, to see if it can be used to predict what will happen under certain new circumstances: 'If in these circumstances I do this, and my hypothesis is true, then that should happen.' She will then design an experiment that aims to prove that the hypothesis is wrong.

At first sight this seems a rather surprising approach: surely the aim is to prove that the hypothesis is true? Consider the two alternatives: either the outcome predicted by the hypothesis does happen, or else it doesn't. If it does happen, then the outcome of the experiment is simply that the list of events that turned out as predicted by the hypothesis has just had one more instance added to it. (Remember, the hypothesis didn't just appear out of thin air; there must have been some event or observation that triggered the train of thought that led to the hypothesis in the first place.) This does not prove the hypothesis to be true, any more than the previous experiments did. If, on the other hand, the predicted event does not happen, then this too requires explanation. It may be that the experiment or the measurements obtained from it were in some way at fault. Experimental results must be scrutinized with great care to ensure, so far as possible, that every influence on the outcome, other than the hypothesis under investigation, has been accounted for and can be safely dismissed as a cause of the outcome.

But it is possible that the hypothesis was wrong. Provided the experiment was well designed and well executed, such an outcome would be fatal to the hypothesis. Back to the drawing-board!

Notice in passing that there is a critical assumption underlying this process: if I recreate *exactly* a given set of circumstances and repeat *exactly* what I did, then the outcome will be the same. However many times our scientist repeats the experiment (provided she has eliminated experimental errors and errors in measurement) it should always give the same result. The universe is reliable and predictable; the task of science is to understand how it works.

The next step in the process is of central importance to the whole business of scientific knowledge. Our scientist submits for publication in a learned journal a paper setting out the story so far. Before publication, this paper is reviewed ('refereed') by acknowledged experts in the field. Their reaction may range from 'Rubbish!', through suggesting some changes in presentation, to comments on the experimental design or procedure. After the referees' comments have been incorporated, the paper is published for the world to read. This part of the process may well be the best way of inviting colleagues to check the experimental design.

Publication will stimulate further responses in the scientific community. Some will want to argue against the conclusions of the paper; others will want to report that this agrees with their own findings (or guesses); others will take up the implicit invitation to repeat the experiment to see if they get the same results. If this yields a succession of positive results, in which the hypothesis is not proved wrong, it (the hypothesis) gains greater acceptance and becomes a theory, a generally accepted account of what happens and why. Most often, however, this hypothesis is only part of a greater story of investigation and discovery. So the body of scientific knowledge grows.

However confidently the theory is accepted as a working explanation and predictive tool, it remains a theory, still open to the possibility that one new experiment calls it into question. This is truly one of the cardinal principles of science: for a theory to be accepted as true, it must have developed, from something like a guess, in the way we have described. As successive experiments fail to prove it wrong, confidence in the theory grows. It must be possible, however, to set up an experiment which could in principle blow the theory entirely out of the water. A belief for which no such experiment could be designed cannot be accepted as scientific truth. To engage seriously with the world of science, one must at some point be prepared to ask the sharp question: 'How could I prove that wrong?' How could this or that theory be demonstrated to be false, in terms that the scientific community would accept as conclusive? Having recognized that this is indeed central to the established procedures of science, it is perhaps a little clearer that science tends to approach faith-based claims with the same sceptical questioning eye, and especially so when the subject matter of the religious claim appears to run counter to a view held widely within the scientific community.

All this has the form of a story: observation, conjecture, experiment, publication, validation of the hypothesis (or else denial, followed either by refinement or by abandonment). It is a story which is re-enacted in scientific laboratories the world over, thousands of times every year. This story *is not the truth* but it has become accepted as a reliable way to advance the search for the truth. *It is the truth* in the sense that (within the scientific paradigm) 'no one comes to the truth except by this route' (compare John 14.6).

Here is another scientific story, this time a particular one. The work of Sir Isaac Newton expressed the firm conviction that the universe is a machine, with all future states calculable, in principle at least, from an initial state together with laws of motion. This conviction (belief?) ruled the day until a French mathematical genius, Henri Poincaré, entered a competition, sponsored by the King of Sweden, in which the winner would be the one who could provide a stable mathematical model of the solar system on the basis of Newton's Laws of Motion. Essentially what was being sought was a set of formulae that, given the known positions of everything at some starting time together with some future date and time, could immediately yield positions and velocities of all the planets and their satellites at that later time. Simply by substituting, for the time variable, an actual time such as '11.37 a.m. on 17 November 3601' we could calculate directly and immediately, from the formulae, the positions of all the planets and their satellites at that distant time. At first sight this sounds rather like the school mathematics problems many of us wrestled with so painfully: a car is travelling at 30 miles per hour; how far has it travelled after 35 minutes? But soon the problem becomes very complex indeed.

These 'Laws' can be used to describe the orbits of *two* bodies under their mutual gravitational attraction – for example, the earth–moon system – by ignoring everything else (remember *Abstraction*?). The King of Sweden clearly assumed that by inviting his contestants to work harder at the mathematics, this simplification could be removed and all dynamic systems could be treated in the same way as the earth–moon system – even the whole solar system. In the end, though, Poincaré didn't solve the problem as set by the king, but the outcome of his investigations was far more significant; he demonstrated that even a system consisting of only *three* bodies cannot be described by a set of formulae of that kind: at some future time *t*, where will all these bodies be, and what will they be doing? It's not a question of the problem being hard; Poincaré demonstrated that it is logically impossible.

This doesn't mean that we *can't* calculate where things will be on 17 November 3601; we just have to do it another way – by calculating where everything will be just a very small interval after the starting time, then using that as the new starting time, repeat the calculation to advance time by the same interval again – and so on until we reach 17 November 3601. The smaller each time-step, the more accurate the final computed result will be.[1] This is of course immensely laborious, and requires vast computing resources. It is this kind of calculation that provides us with weather forecasts. Nevertheless, the word 'deterministic' expresses this idea and captures the notion of the universe as a machine.

As a way of working out the future, however, Poincaré demonstrated that this method depends acutely on those starting conditions; minute variations in the initial conditions could result in immense changes in the outcome. Perhaps the classic expression of this idea is the popular notion that a butterfly flapping its wings in the Amazon rain forest could precipitate a tropical storm on the other side of the Atlantic. Poincaré's investigations resulted in the branch of mathematics now known as *chaos theory*. Unless we are more comprehensively certain than we can possibly be about how things are now, we cannot foretell the future *exactly*. Indeed, things can very easily become chaotic and highly unpredictable. So, is the universe a machine after all?

This too is a story, and in many ways it resembles any detective story. It is an instance of or application of the first story. Stories like this are proving increasingly effective as tools for helping non-scientists to understand something of what science is about

---

1 Strictly, this is an over-simplification. For highly technical reasons, the process of calculation on a computer brings in its own risks of error as well, but by and large these can be managed.

– about how scientists work, and exactly what they claim (and do not claim) for their scientific results. They do not, for the most part, bring the non-scientist to a position where he or she can contribute *as a scientist* to the advancement of knowledge, but it might be hoped that with increasing knowledge will come a greater degree of trust.

So we have scientific stories of two kinds. The first was a kind of *model story* which by its own internal logic constitutes a particular kind of truth; we might call it methodological or procedural truth. As a story it does not embody any facts about the world (except that underlying assumption of reliability and predictability). The second story is an account of truth being uncovered. The story here is quite distinct from the actual truth that was uncovered. It is a fascinating and entertaining human story.

Intriguingly, Poincaré's discovery begins to lay siege to the citadel of scientific method, by raising fundamental questions about that assumption of reliability and predictability.

From a rather different direction we find the phenomenon of quantum theory entering the lists. Here the issue seems to be not *chaos* but *uncertainty*. At the risk of gross over-simplification, it is in principle impossible even to provide a complete description of the initial conditions. The concepts involved here are often so counter-intuitive as to be utterly bizarre – but of course our intuitions are to a great extent conditioned by our experience.

One of the consequences of modern quantum physics is to cast serious doubt on this idea of predicting events; some very small-scale events are inherently unpredictable. This unpredictability on the small scale results in a very small degree of uncertainty about events on the larger scale which are the consequence of vast numbers of small-scale events. In this very limited sense, the view of the universe as a deterministic machine is not sustainable.

Bringing these two notions together – chaos and quantum theory – we find that together they puncture any idea that the universe is a simple machine (as defined above in terms of predictable future states). While such a mechanistic picture can serve us well within limited circumstances (in fact, most of ordinary real life, from snooker to how aeroplanes fly), it is clearly not the answer to everything.

It is possible to make too much of this shift within the world of science. Perhaps the most we can say is that the world disclosed by science has become rather more complicated and (intellectually) hazardous than we had supposed. It follows that (considering this change alone) the position of scientific knowledge has changed slightly in relation to faith knowledge.

While people of faith must be very careful not to leap too gleefully to an unwarranted conclusion about this, it seems to me that there is a rough parallel to be explored between these stories and that of the long exile of the concept of *myth* from much of the Christian world. We shall return to this later.

It is possible to sketch out a contrast between these two types of story, and their different relationships to truth, in a way that may be helpful for our later discussion. Could we conceive of 'truth' in these ways: truth-as-goal and truth-as-journey; truth-as-proposition and truth-as-story; truth-as-result and truth-as-method?

But we cannot leave this fascinating topic without mentioning three other examples of scientific story. The first of these is the story of cosmology. How did the universe begin? How does it work? How big is it? How old is it? Did it even have a beginning? What does the future hold for it? The story which best embodies cosmological truth as currently understood begins with an explosion of energy far bigger than most of us can imagine, which took place about 14 billion years ago. Over the first few seconds of its existence (and remember, in talking of years and seconds we are applying concepts formed in the circumstances with which we are familiar – a 24-hour day on a stable planet) much of this pure energy became transformed into matter – vast clouds of gas consisting of very light atoms such as hydrogen. Gradually this gas clumped together to form galaxies, and eventually stars. As these stars condensed and contracted, heavier atoms were formed – like the ones that make up the things we make and build. As time went by, some of these stars spun off smaller clouds of material. These too condensed, but because they were much smaller they condensed into liquid or solid form, and became planets.

A second story is that of the age and formation of the earth. According to this story, the earth took shape as a globe between four and five billion years ago – an enormous time-span, during which it has been subject to dramatic changes. Tectonic plates jostled for position and so caused vast upheavals of the earth's surface.

The third story is that of evolution by natural selection. Without doubt this story has provoked huge controversy among people of faith – more so in recent decades than it did when it was first circulated by Charles Darwin.

My purpose in mentioning these three stories right now is not to take sides for or against them,[2] but simply to point out that here is a third class of scientific stories, in which *the story is the truth* – at least it is for those who believe them.

Nearly twenty years ago, when I was studying the New Testament during my ordination course, I reached the conclusion that the New Testament was less about conclusions, more about methods. I was encouraged in this view by reading the work of James Dunn,[3] who asserted that the glory of the New Testament is its diversity, its ability to make space, under one roof, for a variety of ways of understanding God, Jesus and the Church. It is deeply sad that so much of the world of faith is marked by an apparent inability to live at ease with other ways of looking at even the same faith-tradition, let alone another. Dunn's conclusion about the New Testament suggests a good principle for faith communities today; the story of faith can be set out as a story of building a house in which all can live.

Narrating the truth

In the previous section we have seen the possibility that a story might convey 'truth' in a way that propositions do not. Contrary, perhaps, to our expectations, stories convey, or contain, or

2 In fact my personal position (as may become clear in due course) is that these are the best explanations on offer, but subject always to the general scientific qualification about being open to question and challenge.

3 J. D. G. Dunn, *Unity and Diversity in the New Testament: An Inquiry into the Character of Earliest Christianity*, London, SCM Press, 1991.

embody, or guide us towards truth in a variety of ways even in such an objective, propositional world as that of science.

Reading the Bible presents its own very particular challenges. It is, for most readers, by far the oldest book they will ever read; its historical setting is remote; its cultural assumptions about what a book is for, and how it should be presented to the world, are quite different from our own. The language of the Creed is somewhat younger – by a few hundred years – but it presents similar difficulties.

Before we plunge into our central task, it is helpful to examine the way we read other books, especially fiction. A good deal of fiction amounts simply to storytelling. The most popular and successful fiction writers do this quite brilliantly and their work gives great pleasure. They have no ulterior motive; they see their task as being, quite simply, to entertain their readers. They have no ambition to win literary prizes, and would probably be astonished if such prizes were ever awarded to them.

There is, however, another kind of fiction, in which – behind the characters and the events – there is a subject, a theme, an issue being opened up for readers to ponder. Many readers will not notice this hidden subject at all; a well-written book of this kind scores on the entertainment scale quite as effectively as does the popular story-novel. But for those inclined to read their novels at a different level, the hidden subject waits ready to be perceived and pondered. The theme may be one of racial prejudice, as in E. M. Forster's *A Passage to India*, or the social mores of nineteenth-century England – an obvious example being Jane Austen's *Pride and Prejudice*.

Even in the so-called historical novel, these two categories may be distinguished, though perhaps the line between them is less sharply drawn. In one the writer's objective is, as before, simply to entertain and perhaps inform. In the other the aim is to view a historical person or situation from a different angle. The academic approach of studying documents, weighing evidence and setting out findings undoubtedly has its place, but the historical novelist blends historical research with storytelling, thus adding entertainment to scholarship – and, incidentally, reaching a wider readership.

So, either we have a historical scenario which is closely based on very specific facts about real characters, or we have a scenario in which the characters and events do not correspond exactly to any real characters and events but which is nevertheless based on an accurate general picture of the historical setting. In either case, one concern of the writer is to help the reader understand the significance of what was going on. She does this by telling the story in a way that is carefully calculated to raise questions about possible interpretations of the bare facts. In its most extreme form, the writer has a theory about what might have happened, and invites the reader to see why she finds the theory so persuasive. In doing so, of course, the historical novelist blurs the distinction between fact and fiction; some might argue that the ordinary reader, who is not a professional historian, may be misled because he or she is unable to make that distinction.

Novels of this second kind – those with a 'hidden subject' – draw a distinction between the *bare facts* about what happened and the *meaning or significance* of what happened. In the hands of a skilful writer, the reader is fully aware of what is happening as he reads: he is being offered a mixture of facts and interpretations, and accepts that he is not being deceived into believing that something happened when it didn't.

All this we accept without debate. We do not need to argue about whether Miss Elizabeth Bennet actually existed in order either to enjoy the story of *Pride and Prejudice*,[4] or to gain a fairly accurate insight into the social circumstances of single gentlewomen in Victorian times. Nor (to change tack slightly) do we need to argue about the factual reality of Lemuel Gulliver, the explorer whose writings purport to describe the bizarre lands of Lilliput and Brobdingnag and the floating island of Laputa. We know Gulliver to be the invention of Jonathan Swift, a clergyman and satirist of the eighteenth century, and we read his *Travels*[5] as a biting satire on the society of his time. How might all this apply to the Bible? The short story of Jonah would be a worthwhile read at this point.

4 J. Austen, *Pride and Prejudice: A Novel*, London, T. Egerton, 1813.

5 J. Swift, J. Chalker and P. Dixon, *Gulliver's Travels*, Harmondsworth, Penguin, 1967.

We have already seen a hint of this in the discussion above on the metaphor of time. In pre-Renaissance painting, important figures (like Jesus) were drawn as larger than other people; apparent size in the painting was a metaphor for importance. Time, too, is used to signify importance: origins and order are situated in a story about the beginning of time; destiny and ultimate importance are signified by being set in a story about the end of time.

Every act of storytelling takes place in a particular context, against the background of a particular set of historical circumstances. Writers and readers, storytellers and hearers, must have *something* in common if the storytelling is to communicate anything. Obviously, the more they have in common, the more effective the communication will probably be. While it may be most effective if the storyteller and her audience share the same point of view, and respond to stories in similar ways, that is not in fact essential. It would be good, however, if they could at least understand one another.

There have been many periods in history when stories have been told, quite deliberately, in an indirect form, as a way of not arousing suspicions. The stories of Jonathan Swift, which have already been mentioned, are examples of such cryptic literature, but one does not need to look far to find modern parallels. During the Soviet era in the USSR there was a thriving literature of anti-government satire carefully crafted so as to be entertaining to everyone while concealing its true purpose. Here, understanding was carefully managed by the writer, so as not to ruffle feathers in the establishment.

In our discussion of religious ideas, the word 'sacred' appears often. In everyday speech this word carries many meanings, ranging from the factual – for example, 'relating to God or to religion' – to a rather disparaging meaning – for example, something is a *sacred cow* if it is viewed (irrationally) as being above criticism. It is possible for these two very different uses to interact with one another, so a person of genuine religious sensitivities may feel deeply offended when a word (or a name) they cherish is used without the reverence they would wish to see attached to it.

A cynic might, at this point, be forgiven the thought that we are now in the realm of Humpty Dumpty, who used words exactly as he pleased; he cared nothing for the idea that to be at all useful (in conversation, say) the meaning of a word must be agreed by all participants, otherwise chaos, confusion and misunderstanding will reign. But perhaps we are now in a different world, where I cannot 'lock down' the meaning and significance of a word and expect everyone else to handle that word in the same way that I do.

So, what might the word 'sacred' mean, and why am I so anxious to explain it at this point? Taking the second question first, I believe that protagonists on all sides would do well to try to understand one another better, and in particular to understand why they hold their particular views with such defensive ferocity.

To answer the first question, I need to tell a little personal story.

Shakespeare has Hamlet say to Horatio, 'There are more things in heaven and earth . . . than are dreamt of in your philosophy.' Most of us are familiar with the idea that there are particular places, particular pieces of music, particular words or pictures that remind us of the 'more things'. I remember vividly an experience that took me completely by surprise. At the time, the Stanley Spencer Gallery in Cookham, Berkshire, was hosting an exhibition of Spencer's landscape painting. As I entered the gallery I saw, high on the opposite wall and slightly to my left, a painting that held me transfixed for quite some time – if pressed, I would say it must have been about twenty minutes. I wasn't just looking at it; I was held by it. Many times I have tried to analyse what was going on in my head to provoke this reaction, but in the end I am forced to acknowledge that whatever it was lay outside the realms of wonderment at Spencer's composition or technique. I was driven to ask myself, 'What is the *landscape* saying to me through this painting?'

Such experiences do not fall only into the sphere of religion or poetry. Richard Dawkins has often spoken of a similar experience when a new scientific insight dawns upon him. Moses' experience with the 'burning bush' and Elijah's with the 'still, small voice' must surely share much with mine of Spencer's painting and Dawkins' Eureka moments. In saying this, of course, I respect Dawkins' right to interpret his experience in his own way. I cannot crudely equate his with mine, either in the Stanley Spencer Gallery or when celebrating the Eucharist in church. All I dare say is that there seems to be some kinship between them. And all I can ask of my own readers is that they give one another the same courtesy.

Of course, it isn't only, or always, a painting that produces this sort of result. It might be a place, or a person, or a poem, or any one of a number of experiences. For my own part I can certainly identify a few special places where I can very easily experience this sense of awe, and of connectedness with a world that is so often merely the backdrop to my existence. This is what I mean by the *sacred*; some may choose not to accept this meaning – perhaps this sort of experience just doesn't happen to them. But I think it will help them, in reading the rest of this book, if they have some clue as to what religious believers might mean when they use such a word. As we shall soon see, there are other words that attempt to express the same sort of idea from a slightly different perspective: take, for example, the word 'holy'.

Close to the beginning of the Lord's Prayer there is a phrase 'hallowed [= holy] be thy name'. Part of the meaning behind this phrase is that we should treat with special reverence experiences of the sacred, and the contexts in which they happen to us. At this point we might reasonably ask, 'Why should we treat these experiences with reverence?' After all, Jesus' instruction in prayer was set in a context in which everybody belonged to the community of faith; that was, in part, why the Roman occupation was so deeply resented. To 'treat God's name as holy' was precisely a key component of what it meant to be a member of that community. In our time, however, we are free to choose whether or not we are members of a believing community. Is there any possible resonance between this very specific religious usage and other human experiences?

I remember once attending a lecture at the university where I was a member of the academic staff – a lecture about the moon, from which astronauts had only recently returned. The object of the greatest interest, which held people in rapt wonder, was a small sealed perspex box. In it was a piece of moon rock – just a few grams in weight. It was not dangerous in any way; no one was inclined to fear it or pray to it or anything like that. But it was *different*, in a way that clearly evoked wonder and a kind of secular reverence. In a way, I suppose it symbolized, to that audience, the threshold of space exploration that humanity was in the process of crossing, the dawn of a new era in human development. This sense of awe reflected, perhaps, a growing awareness that we, humanity, were inching open the door to a vast unknown region; as we took that step we had little idea what technologies we would need to develop, what precautions we might need to take, what rewards beckoned, and what dangers threatened. Although that is not a definition of the holy, it may give a fair idea of what the word 'holy' means in a religious context. Clearly, the words 'holy' and 'sacred' are very closely related.

This need for reverence towards experiences of the sacred and the places where such experiences happen finds expression in dire warnings of what will happen if the sacredness of those places or things is not respected. It is typical of the Bible – especially the early part of it which Christians call 'The Old Testament' – that instead of setting forth propositions about God, the Bible tells stories. Often these stories reflect challenge, like Moses' encounter with the 'burning bush' in Exodus 3. Sometimes they are shocking, as when heavenly visitors convinced a childless elderly couple (Abraham and Sarah) that they would soon have a child of their own. Occasionally, however, these stories come across to us as – to put it mildly – divine heavy-handedness of a most extreme kind. The case of Uzziah is a good example.[6] He was involved in the procession carrying a sacred object (the Ark of the Covenant – an ornate chest containing the stone tablets on which the Ten Commandments were written) to its new home on an ox-cart, when the oxen stumbled. Uzziah steadied the Ark with his hands, and for this error he 'was struck dead' by God. Perhaps this is one reason why the God of the Old Testament has such a bad press. Looked at another way, however, these grisly stories take on a different flavour. Uzziah probably died of natural causes, but this was explained by the writer as the anger of God. After all, God is all-powerful, so whatever happened must be God's responsibility

6 See 2 Samuel 6.6–11.

– especially when such a sacred object as the Ark was involved. Again, we see a story that has been coloured in the telling and re-telling by a set of views about God and the sacred. Of itself, this doesn't make those views any more, or less, worthy or tenable; it merely provides grounds on which we can assess them.

These, then, are some of the ingredients of the 'cake' that is the Bible. We need to read very carefully to understand how the stories took their present shape, and what we can say about their meaning.

The Creed as story

The Apostles' Creed begins with God and the creation, and it ends with 'the life everlasting'. In between, the text tells us, concisely, of the central elements in the Christian story. It is not, therefore, simply a list of propositions to be believed. The list is certainly structured, in two ways.

First, it reflects the distinctively Christian understanding of God as Trinity. It does not attempt, however, to elaborate upon this, explain it, or justify it. It is taken as given, as the framework upon which everything we may say about God is to be hung.

Second, it has this story form. In the long central section about Jesus it begins with a statement of Jesus' nature (God's only Son, our Lord), and goes on to summarize Jesus' life-story, beginning with his conception and ending with his role in judgement.

'Story' is a form we can identify with. A story enables us to place ourselves in the action. A story is marked by high points and low points, crises, dilemmas and resolutions. A story involves people, their human situations and their responses to those situations. A story may or may not be set in the reader's own time, but the reader will be able to see in the story enough of her own context to be able to share in its action, disappointments, shocks, cruelties, heroism, endurance and destiny.

Earlier, I suggested a simple classification of scientific stories according to three models: the story as a programme for action, like the 'hypothesis, experiment, publish' story; the story as a stirring romance, a tale of inquiry leading to a conclusion, like the story of Poincaré and chaos theory; and the story which *is* the truth, of which I gave three examples: cosmology, the formation of the earth, and the evolution of life.

In what way, if any, does the Creed story resemble these models? Some would certainly want to insist that it most resembles the third model: the story *is* the truth. I would want to argue that much is to be gained by viewing the Creed as a stirring romance, a tale of heroic devotion and unswerving commitment, and with an unmistakable transcendent dimension.

Why might it help to view the Creed in this way? I suggest it would be helpful in the following ways.

It is surely pointless to deny that, when people are invited to recite the Creed during a service, there is for many a suspension of disbelief, precisely because they see the Creed as a set of propositions to be assented to; they are given no choice but to assent. If they retain their private uncertainties, it will be hard for them to resist the conclusion that the whole thing is a preposterous sham in which they can no longer take part with integrity. See the Creed as a story, however, and the shackles of belief are relaxed somewhat, giving those who are saying it some freedom to decide the ways and the extent to which they can identify with it.

To this suggestion there is an objection. Parents whose children are learning life's basic moral rules will be familiar with the injunction, 'Don't tell stories!' Used in this sense, stories are fiction; worse, they are *deliberately misleading* fiction. The same parents, however, will take great delight in telling stories at their children's bedtime. The distinction between these two uses of the word 'story' lies in the realm of the relationship between story and truth which we have already explored in Chapter 2. Where in the popular mind *story* is equivalent to *deliberately misleading fiction*, it is understandable that there will be resistance to the suggestion that the Creed is a story.

A second way in which it may be helpful to read the Creed as a story, is that it invites us to identify ourselves and our own stories with it. In a few words the Creed summarizes the entire Christian story of God's steadfast love and self-giving in offering humanity rescue from its self-inflicted nemesis. It does so by reminding us of the life and ministry of Jesus.

In pre-literate medieval Europe, churches were decorated with frescoes, paintings and statues which depicted in visual form the story of human disaster and salvation. The Creed provided a concise and memorable form of words that people could internalize and which would live with them in their daily life. The Creed was their podcast. They saw its meaning echoed in their daily experience of hardship and reward, of faithfulness and abandonment. They encountered its heart in seeing Mass celebrated. In short, the Creed, along with these other influences, will have helped them internalize their faith-commitment.

We in the twenty-first century, however, are bombarded with stories. Our iPods are loaded with story and music, information and amusement, drawn from an immense variety of sources. Certainly these influences do not add up to a reinforcement of a Christian message – and in this age of choice it is hardly arguable that they should be so uniform; we have had enough of totalitarian ideologies. But for any who want to do so, the Creed offers a story to which believers can respond with heartfelt joy: 'This story I can and do identify with; this story helps me make sense of my world and my life.'

What, then, of myth, that particular symbolic story which we encountered in the previous chapter? What is the characteristic distinguishing feature of myth by which we can compare it with stories of other kinds? My answer to this question is that myth does not contain the truth; it does not offer a procedure for arriving at the truth; it does not describe the journey of other people to the truth (except perhaps incidentally). Rather, myth is a story which invites us to identify ourselves with its characters and its events, to see our story traced in its course. Such identification does not of course amount to an exact correspondence of one of the elements of the myth to the elements of our own story. Instead, we may see it as an invitation to a conversation in which we ourselves move in and out of the symbolic story and reflect upon the ever-changing climate of our own experience. Truth is discovered as the conversation proceeds – which may take many years.

A final note

We have spent quite some time on a few of the many ways in which we speak indirectly about our subject. Sometimes this is because, although we could put direct language to work quite successfully, indirect metaphoric or poetic language actually does the job better. Sometimes a story expresses our meaning better than a bald series of statements. There is, after all, a sense in which the Creed is not designed as a conveyor of information, but rather as an expression of a value-system through the re-telling of a story. The subject matter of the Creed is God, about which many theologians (and others) believe we are not in a position, strictly, to say anything at all – certainly not in direct language. This provides us with a second reason for resorting to indirect language.

In writing this book I have tried to begin by using metaphoric and other symbolic language as the language of first resort. For this decision I offer a third reason: if anyone were to pick up this book and read it who is not already a Christian, I believe that such an approach may help them to read on and find that they can at least understand a little of the way some Christians might think. But I have found it impossible to stick rigidly to this strategy. Sooner or later the committed Christian preacher in me wins the day and I find I have shifted towards the standard set of Christian assumptions about how to describe our faith. For this I do not apologize. Sooner or later, whether the content of the Creed is held to be metaphorical or literal, we have to respond to it with our whole heart, not just as a set of propositions that we are at liberty to accept or reject in the light of the evidence.

And therein lies my final defence. I have argued that direct, literal speech about God (among other subjects) is impossible, because we do not have direct access to a description of God. Indeed, the very idea is absurd because our minds are limited. H. G. Wells once wrote: 'our imagination is limited by our experience'. All we have is 'figures of speech' – which is precisely what Jesus' friends complained about for much of the time: he spoke in parables, rather than more directly.

Jesus was no fool. He was, I suspect, well aware that to offer a set of propositions about God and invite people to accept them as true, was to run the risk that his hearers might suppose that to believe means *no more than* to accept those propositions as true. What he sought, on the contrary, was a transformation of heart and action as well as of mind. The propositions would have been just a framework on which to hang those transformations and commitments.

So, to anyone who turns away from this book in dismay, dismissing metaphor as insubstantial and valueless, I respond thus. I have no better way of discussing the subject than through metaphor. But I believe what the metaphors are attempting to say, I accept what the metaphors are attempting to describe.

4

What is a Creed and Why Did They Come into Existence?

Four 'b's

This chapter is in some senses a digression. While it is instructive to learn something of the controversies which were the birth-pangs of the distinctively Christian pattern of believing, in the context of this book this is background information for our real project: to explore what believing might mean in the twenty-first century.

Of all world religions, Christianity is arguably the most complex as a collection of ideas. The very existence of the Creed is testimony to the weight the Church has attached to right belief. Other religions are much more modest in terms of the beliefs to which they expect their adherents to subscribe. Instead, they attach greater weight to other aspects of the religious life. A number of Christian writers have pointed out that there are various understandings of what it means to be a Christian, which we may characterize simply as *believing*, *behaving* and *belonging*, depending on whether belief or conduct or mutual commitment is held to be the most important. To these three 'b's we may add a fourth: *becoming*, which reflects the dynamic character of all religious commitments.

These three – believing, behaving and belonging – are interrelated, of course, but faith communities differ in the way they view them. For example, during the process of being received into full membership of a religious community like a church, hesitancy or uncertainty about belief might be tolerated, but full membership would presuppose unreserved commitment to common beliefs.

Expectations about conformity of conduct, too, might vary from one community to another, even when the community is perfectly clear about the standard being upheld as desirable.

Advocates of the *believing* model assert the primacy of subscribing to a common set of beliefs. In the first century the Christian community's faith – its 'confession' – consisted of one simple statement: Jesus is Lord. As the Christian centuries unfolded, new Christians were taught using a credal formula which was based on a series of lectures by the local bishop. After an examination, during which they were questioned about their faith, candidates were baptized and/or confirmed. The common basis of this teaching evolved over the centuries, leaving traces in the form of the three principal creeds of which we have the texts, and culminating in what we now know as the Apostles' Creed. This process of evolution has left traces of earlier credal formulations; while the Church cherishes these as historic documents, they are very rarely studied except by professional scholars. We shall return to these important words later, in Chapter 10.

Controversies behind the creeds

The primary role and function of the Apostles' Creed was, then, as a concise summary of the bishop's introductory lectures for new Christians.

In the meantime, especially during the fourth century CE, debates raged about a number of apparently arcane ideas, including the following:

1. The human world is so flawed, the material world so capricious and meaningless; how can God have pronounced it good?
2. How is Jesus related to the transcendent idea of God?
3. What exactly do we mean by resurrection?

So furious were these debates that the Church threatened to fall apart entirely. Denunciations of one prelate by another are strewn through the calendar of the first four centuries.[1] Great confer-

1 It is interesting to view the present turmoil in the churches alongside these much earlier controversies. There is nothing new under the sun!

ences were held in which scholars argued their various cases with great passion – because they regarded the issues as of vital importance. These conferences hardly matched the conventions of what we would now call the rules of debate. The British House of Commons is sometimes dismissively referred to as a 'bear-pit', but it is a very refined tea party compared to what happened at some of these Church conferences or Councils. The underlying purpose of these Councils was, in fact, to define – in terms of belief – what it means to be a Christian. Those of the minority opinion were required to recant; the alternative open to them was to be dismissed as heretics and excommunicated – banished from the Christian family.

A great deal of very deep thinking took place around the first of these questions – and still does. The central issue is the nature of the world, both physical and human. The Christian view is that God made it and it is good. The heretical view is that the world is the embodiment of evil, as opposed to the spiritual realm which is entirely good. From this source there has come a long stream of thought that divides everything into good (i.e. 'like us'), and evil (i.e. 'like them'). It did much to shape the way in which the Church responded to the second question, as we shall now see.

The principal bone of contention in these prolonged debates was the second in the list: How is Jesus related to the transcendent idea of God? We shall say more about this when we come to the section of the Creed that begins, 'I believe in Jesus Christ'. But it is worth pausing here a moment to outline this particular issue. The central Christian claim about Jesus is that he is both God and man; he is the perfect representation of God, *and* he is the perfect representative of humanity. This formula didn't emerge quickly, nor was there ready agreement about it. Two groups within the Christian community argued their opposing – and essentially negative – conclusions about Jesus, each group denying one component of the formula.

One group, called the Arians (named after Arius, the man who was the chief exponent of this view), denied that Jesus could be divine. He was, they argued, a unique man who carried out a special divine commission and enjoyed special divine favour, but he was not God. This strand of thought emerged from the belief that

God is unchangeable; Jesus is represented in the Gospels as a person who grows, learns and changes. Hence Jesus cannot be God. In the terms in which we have expressed it here, Jesus cannot be both human and transcendent. Battle raged for many years around this counter-claim, and indeed played a part in the ultimate dissolution of the Roman Empire by alienating those barbarian tribes who had become Christian.

The other group held the opposite view, but for a very similar reason. Jesus only *appeared* to be human; in reality he remained God – just God – throughout his life. The argument ran like this: the physical and human world is so corrupt and evil that it is simply unacceptable to claim that God (in the person of Jesus) actually became part of it. To this belief the name Docetism was attached; the Greek verb *dokein* means *to seem*.

To cut a long story short, these debates resulted in the Nicene Creed of 381 CE. Relative to the Apostles' Creed, this is a rather more comprehensive and detailed document, designed not for instructing new converts but for defending the Church against heresy. In short, therefore, the creeds became not just the banner under which Christians rally, they took on also the character of the razor-wire that surrounds and protects the Christian encampment. We can read the Nicene Creed today without really being aware of the nature and ferocity of the debates that were going on and whose results found expression in some of its apparently innocuous phrases.

In fairness, it has to be said that this metaphorical razor-wire serves not only to keep heretics *out*; it also keeps *in* the orthodox faithful – those who believe 'correctly'. At first sight this may seem draconian and dictatorial, but (so some would argue) it is surely reasonable enough to insist that shared membership entails shared beliefs and values – at least to some extent. In particular, of course, to ensure that the views now pronounced heretical do not find their way back into the company of believers. *Believing* is a precondition of full *belonging*. In today's world of mutually aware alternative cultures, such shared beliefs and values are often seen as little more than consumer choices. This strengthens the impression that religious belief has at its heart (or perhaps better, *in its head*) nothing of substance.

So, we have seen two perspectives on the purpose of a creed: one is rooted in the believing model for which a creed acts as instructor, the other in the belonging model for which a creed acts as boundary marker. Originally the (Apostles') Creed was first spoken – or assented to – by a candidate for baptism or confirmation as the climax of a period of study and instruction in the faith which was based upon the Creed. According to this view, the Creed was not just a kind of theological 'title-deed', kept in a safe. Rather, it was an everyday working document used in explaining the Christian faith.

David Harned has taken this line of argument further,[2] claiming that the creed is rather an 'identity avowal', a profession of belonging that implies sharing in the community's belief. But it is more, Harned claims, than simply a response to the question, 'Is he one of us?' He writes this:

> 'I believe' is primarily an acknowledgement that the self stands in a relationship to God, sees itself always in the light of God's inescapable presence, subordinating to this all other elements of its understanding of itself, and therefore derives from this situation its own sense of identity.

But the (Nicene) Creed evolved also as a boundary marker around correct belief. Over time the Church had wrestled painfully with a number of subtle assertions, particularly about God, and Jesus, and the Holy Spirit. The legacy to today's Church is a catalogue of heresies (= *false teachings*), and a series of creeds that define what is, and what is not, orthodox (= *correct teaching*) Christian belief. Despite the labours of the ecumenical Councils, these heresies have not died out. From time to time they re-surface in the records of division in the Church, the formation of sects and parties. But that is another story.

There are difficulties with each of these views, the instructive and the defensive. There is much that the Creed does not say which we would now regard as central to Christian self-understanding. In the third part of this book, we pick up this thread.

---

2 D. B. Harned, *Creed and Personal Identity: The Meaning of the Apostles' Creed*, Philadelphia, Fortress Press, 1981, p. 19.

The language of the Creed

While most students of the Apostles' Creed see in it a set of propositions, the thoughtful reader may notice that its overall structure resembles a story. It begins with God and affirms that the world was created; it goes on to tell a story about Jesus, his birth, his life, the manner of his death, and quite a bit about what happened afterwards (and also about what is yet to happen). We'll come to those details in due course. But for now we notice simply that the form in which it is cast resembles that of a story. So, it is possible to receive it and identify with it both as propositional and as story; these alternatives are not inherently hostile to one another.

A provocative writer of the mid-twentieth century, Marshall McLuhan, coined a phrase that became famous: the medium is the message. Even here, the medium is (at least part of) the message. Christian believing begins with the idea of a story, a narrative with a beginning, a middle, a crux, a resolution and an end. In talking about their beliefs, Christians want to state loud and clear that there is meaning and purpose underlying it all. We express this fundamentally by telling a story about it. The life of the cosmos cannot be reduced to an endless cycle of getting and spending, birth and death, evolution and extinction of species, of stars burning all their nuclear fuel in one final explosion before dwindling to a dark, dense ball.

Like all good stories, this one invites us to identify ourselves with the action on the stage, to see our life (birth, education, career, getting, spending, dying) as part of that bigger story. Indeed, the theme of transcendence that runs through this book finds its place even here in the story-form of the Creed, because the Creed invites us to see that the way we transcend the ordinariness of our lives is to understand them as part of that bigger story. It may even be acceptable to regard the Creed as a symbolic story.

At the level of detail, however, the Creed fills that story with ideas that come from a different mould. They are (or appear to be) propositions, assertions that are either true or false. This is where things get more difficult. How do we work with those 'propositions'? Are we simply to take them at face value? Or are there other options for us to think about?

The Creed talks a lot about God and Jesus, using language that seems far removed from ordinary everyday conversation. This sense of strangeness is inevitable, and not just because the Creed is talking about God and Jesus; it's strange also because the Creed is addressing profound questions about the meaning of life which, in ordinary everyday life, we don't often find it easy to talk about. So it is inevitable that the language and the ideas seem a bit odd. You wouldn't expect a television engineer to explain your fuzzy picture without using *some* specialized language; the same is true of whatever it is the Creed is about.

We shall see that the underlying idea is that of God, the transcendent, the kind of feelings we get when looking at a sunset, or listening to a love song, being alongside a person in a cancer clinic who's been given the all-clear – or being at the bedside of someone who's dying. This sensation is far more, we're claiming, than a faint memory of something. It's a genuine guide to a level of reality that for most of the time barely touches our consciousness.

For Christian believers, a person who lived 2,000 years ago is somehow central to how we grapple with this idea of the transcendent. Jesus gives us clues as to how to live life each day in the knowledge that moments of transcendence are never far away, and that we will be able to respond to them better if our lives are ordered according to the values he proclaimed. To believe in him is to believe that he does represent this 'God' idea more perfectly than anyone else has ever done, and to commit ourselves fully to 'doing things his way'.

The Creed begins to answer these questions by referring to Jesus as the Son of God, but that answer draws us into territory that is very unfamiliar to twenty-first-century people. Indeed, it has never been easy to explain these ideas; we're always talking obliquely, indirectly, hinting at things rather than stating things explicitly – precisely because we *cannot* speak of them explicitly. It is the language of poetry, of metaphor. To describe Jesus as Son of God is to use language that is sitting exactly on the border between the literal and the metaphorical.

We must be careful, however, not to suppose that the indirect nature of metaphor implies a lack of precision. Metaphoric language can be precise in the way it illuminates a problem of understanding, though not in the way that a scientist or engineer might talk of precision in his or her daily life. When I learned physics as a schoolboy I was reminded at least once a term not to write down a number to more places of decimals than my measuring technology (or experimental skill) would justify. My wooden 'ruler', with its graduations in tenths of an inch along one edge, or millimetres along the other, could never yield a measurement in millimetres accurately to better than about half a millimetre. I could write down in my notebook a measurement of, say, 7.649 mm – but the moment I confessed to reaching this conclusion with my ruler, I would be laughed out of the laboratory. Where a metaphor can be precise is quite a different matter. It is precise if its result is an unusual sense of illumination or understanding – a Eureka moment. A slight change of wording would result in a less effective metaphor.

Clearly, this evaluation of metaphors introduces an element of subjectivity – the response to a metaphor is highly personal. What rings bells for me may not ring bells for you. This is precisely what science is trying to eliminate; if the measurement depends on the mood or temperament of the observer, then a key element is lost. Suppose another observer carries out the same experiment and gets the same result (in terms of what he has written in his laboratory notebook). Unless we are clear that in both cases the measurements are truly objective, we cannot argue that the second experimenter confirms (or not) the findings of the first. In the case of metaphors that try to describe the indescribable, we are left with the possibility of conversation between two observers, in the course of which they might (or might not) find themselves 'talking the same language' about their experiences or beliefs.

Because it is so indirect, this sort of language enables us to say (or suggest) much more than we could with the more exact language of science – a point often overlooked by protagonists of options 1 and 2 (see above, Chapter 2). In fact, following the phenomenal rise in the explanatory powers of science from the sixteenth century onwards, Christians have felt under pressure to express their faith in similar terms – as if Christian belief were about facts and figures in a scientific sense. Christians, in a word, have been drawn onto science's battleground.

To the literal interpretation, one can say only 'Yes' or 'No'. With the metaphorical, one can explore, discover and learn. That is why I find the metaphorical more helpful to the expression of faith.

The Church reflects a range of views spanning options 2 and 3, discussed in Chapter 2. We are involved in a perpetual tension between literal and metaphorical language, and it is all too easy for anyone – believer or not – to lose her bearings, and believe she is in one linguistic territory when in fact she is in the other. If this is difficult for a committed believer, how much harder may it be for a non-believer trying to make sense of faith?

We have linked metaphor with poetry, but this is not to equate one with the other. Certainly poetry employs metaphor very heavily, but the value of metaphor is not confined to the poetic.

Part 2

The Content of Belief

We have remarked that the Apostles' Creed took shape over many centuries, emerging in its present form, after very long debate, in about the eighth century of the Christian era. It was during this period that the Church was also able to clarify a number of important matters in the Nicene Creed.

The Church split into two major groupings, the Eastern and the Western; the Western Church adopted the Apostles' Creed and the Nicene Creed, while the Eastern Church 'begged to differ' on some important issues and went its own way. Within the Western (initially the Roman Catholic) Church these two formulations of Christian belief have grown to pre-eminence.

This part of the book follows closely the structure of the Apostles' Creed. Chapters 5, 6 and 7 deal with God, Jesus and the Holy Spirit respectively.

Some readers will be puzzled about the way in which Chapter 6 is subdivided. Please refer back to Chapter 1 for discussion of metaphor, myth and symbolic language. In the postmodern world the word 'myth' has become synonymous with 'falsehood' – anything which is a myth must be banished from public discussion. The earlier notion of a myth is that it is a symbolic story that we can identify with, and in which we can find help as we navigate the hazards of life. Subdividing the story of Jesus in this way creates a framework for our exploration. You may not need this; if you find it helpful, it will have served its purpose.

5

God

'I believe in God,'

There's nothing like being thrown in at the deep end, is there? This creed does not allow us to hide behind anyone else: *I* believe in God. What does it mean to believe; and what do we mean by 'God'? What can we *possibly* mean by 'God'?

There are, of course, various answers to this question according to which of views 1, 2 and 3 we subscribe to. 'Old man in the sky' is one; 'Architect of the universe' might be another; 'Supreme Being' yet a third. All of these have one serious defect: they conjure up a picture of a 'thing' that can be found somewhere, a 'someone' who does things. We'll come on to the 'Architect' in a later section. The third of these definitions, 'Supreme Being', is perhaps the best, and at the same time the least helpful because what it says is so vague. Furthermore, whatever their defects, each one of them is saying something that we need to factor into our notion of God.

What does the picture of God as an 'Old man in the sky' do for you? It may say something rather unpleasant about our society that we refer to an old man – perhaps a grey-haired old man – as dismissively as we often do. Ours is a society that is apt to regard old people as worthless, irrelevant, stupid, ignorant, out of touch. Little wonder, then, that this picture of God furnishes us with a convenient excuse for marginalizing God completely. God may or may not be dead, but we've put him in a care home where he can't interfere with our lives – the way we bring up our children, how we vote, where we go on holiday, and so on.

Right now in many parts of the world, old age is still a sign of wisdom; it evokes reverence and respect rather than scorn. This was also true for earlier generations of our own society. Today's dismissive view of the old is perhaps the anomaly, not the norm, when the big historical perspective is taken into account. We must acknowledge, however, that in societies where the old are treated with reverence, the idea of the end of life may not have carried the implications it does today, of senility, dementia or other forms of incapacity. Life expectancy would probably be much less than in our own communities. It may be that for the majority of elderly people, wisdom and articulate experience could survive intact until a brief final illness or an accident.

Of course, that is not the only perspective on age. Grandpa (I'm glad to report, from personal experience!) is still sometimes seen as a friendly figure who has time to play or read when parents don't, offers treats now and again, has interesting stories to tell, is generally a good thing, and can discreetly disappear when no longer wanted.

In both these images there is a very small measure of truth and a large helping of fantasy. We do well to remember that whatever image of God we may have is inadequate, especially if we haven't revised that image since we were very young. It is one of the more depressing aspects of Christian ministry to discover how many adult church members are content with a picture of God that would be rejected by many children. Perhaps it's simply because they don't have the motivation, the means or the permission to bring themselves 'up to speed' with God.

The 'Supreme Being' image is perhaps the best, at least to begin with, because it is clearly not afraid of wandering outside our familiar human world. Can we distinguish between those two words: 'Supreme' and 'Being'? They say, after all, two very different things about our belief in 'God'.

First, then, the word 'Supreme'. It suggests a concept that actually embraces and includes every other concept, an idea than which no other idea is bigger, more all-embracing, more complete, or more 'satisfactory'.

That was a rather philosophical sort of definition, and for many it may not provide much of an explanation. We need to try a different tack.

Some years ago the bookstands at airports would invariably have on display a book called *In Search of Excellence*,[1] written by Tom Peters and Rob Waterman. Peters was a 'management guru', an expert on management who still tours the world giving seminars on how to do better in business, as a manager or a salesperson. His audience was full of people who wanted to do better, to excel, to reach beyond themselves. For them, that was – and for many it still is – the primary motivating factor. It's what induces them to get up every morning and go to work.

Every year, at countless games all over the world, athletes strive to do their best – indeed to outshine even their own best. Victory over others is, of course, an easily identifiable goal, but victory over oneself plays its part too – to attain a 'personal best' in one's chosen sporting discipline.

This is true of other fields of human activity too. Musicians, writers and artists are all striving for excellence, but of a kind that is not quite so easily characterized, simply because no performance can ever be quite perfect; perfection is, if you like, the 'absolute' of excellence.

A word that is sometimes used to describe the work of outstanding artists and musicians is 'transcendent'. It suggests a performance of surpassing excellence, one that in some way lifts the receptive listener above himself, out of his (or of course her) world into a realm of inspired exaltation. The related word 'transported' is sometimes found as a near-synonym.

Whether there is any link to the Peters and Waterman book is not clear, but in many fields, from sport and the arts to ferret breeding (!), there is now a movement (or perhaps movements) under the generic head 'The Pursuit of Excellence'.

The word 'transcendence' has also been used in an educational context to denote an awareness of the bigger picture[2] and to refer

1 T. J. Peters and R. H. Waterman, *In Search of Excellence: Lessons From America's Best-run Companies*, London, Profile, 2004.

2 See H. Sharron and M. Coulter, *Changing Children's Minds: Feuerstein's Revolution in the Teaching of Intelligence*, Birmingham, Imaginative Minds, 1996. On page 203 there is a questionnaire on mediated learning; see Topic 2: Transcendence. In this book on the education of children with learning difficulties, these authors employ the word 'transcendence' to signify the idea that a lesson is not an end in itself, but fits into a bigger picture – the whole course,

to wider awareness in a general sense: that this activity in which we are now engaged does fit into a larger programme of activity; that this turmoil in which I am now tangled can find meaning in a larger context.

These meanings can give us a clue as to how to approach the idea of God. When, through the medium of a musical performance, a poem, a sunset, we are transported to such a realm, 'where' exactly is it that we 'go'? Is the word 'go' even remotely appropriate for such an experience? Clearly the words 'transported' and 'go' are metaphors.

It may seem on the face of things that transcendence is unequivocally a good and comfortable thing. This is not the case, however. The idea of transcendence is also associated with episodes of great pain and grief, or with art and music that evoke such moods. One writer referred to such experiences as 'living at depth', implying that, for most of the time, most of us are skating merrily over the surface of things. The depths – and the heights – are for us, to some degree, alien environments like the depths of the oceans or the rarefied atmosphere of the high Himalayas. We cannot survive them without engaging parts of our inner being that in normal times lie dormant – and idle.

Many people believe that this notion of transcendence is purely a mental state, corresponding to no external reality whatsoever. The only meaning of transcendence they can find is one that lies firmly 'between the ears'. If that is so, there seems little point in attempting to communicate with other people who have had a similar experience; little or no point in attempting to get a grip on it, because it is no more than a mental state – and perhaps a deluded one! I cannot deny that this position may be found to be the correct one, but if it is, I have to confess to real difficulty with the problem of how to live as a human being.

In affirming that 'we believe in God' we are asserting our belief in the possibility of transcendence, that there is a 'best' worth striving for, that there is a 'bigger picture' into which our activities fit, that there is a story into which we can fit the stories of our lives. (But see the section on Postmodernism in Chapter 2.)

---

or the whole curriculum. Skills learned or knowledge acquired in earlier lessons can be applied here.

Akbar Ahmed writes[3] of his namesake Jalaluddin Muhammad Akbar[4] that he made a pilgrimage to a Muslim shrine at Ajmer, in India, to pray for the gift of a son. He went as a supplicant, a posture which Ahmed describes as 'an effective way to check the ego'. This is another manifestation of transcendence. Even a great emperor stands as a supplicant.

There is another possible meaning for the word 'God': it may denote 'that which we take with the utmost seriousness'. Sometimes we do this rationally, sometimes with the best reasoning power we can muster (which for some of us is 'not a lot!'), and sometimes on a hunch. What exactly we take with the utmost seriousness may be rock music, the state of the environment, economics, personal satisfaction through consumption, our career, our key human relationships – or indeed myriad other things. The point is that, for us, whatever it may be, it outranks everything else. This brings us neatly back to the idea of transcendence.

Now we must turn to the word 'being'. When used of the transcendent, this is a very dangerous word indeed. Think very carefully about what this word conjures up for you. I would hazard a guess that for most people it would be essential, for this word 'being' to be properly applied, that what it is applied to should be alive. We may talk of a flower meadow just 'being', but when we think carefully, we are referring not only to the plant life comprising the meadow, but also to the myriad living things for whom that meadow is home – or, in the case of a barn owl, a fox or a hedgehog, a hunting-ground.

Living things are finite and have boundaries. We each inhabit a body with a highly sensitive boundary: our skin. We also inhabit a territory, which we might define either as the space about which our senses can give us direct information, or the collec-

---

3 Akbar Ahmed, former High Commissioner of Pakistan in Britain, and a passionate advocate of better understanding and mutual respect between the great world faiths. His book (A. Ahmed, *Journey into Islam*, Washington DC, Brookings Institution Press, 2007) presents a remarkable appraisal of the present condition of the Muslim world and the West's prolonged mishandling of relations with it.

4 Mughal Emperor, 1556–1605, and himself a great innovator with regard to religious tolerance. He did indeed have a son, and the birth was widely attributed to his prayerful devotion.

tion of such spaces that make up our daily round of commuting, shopping, regular journeys and so on. Anything that happens outside that territory we know of only indirectly, through other people's reports. Our life advances through stages, from conception to burial or cremation, accumulating and discarding memories, achieving and failing, loving and being loved, being popular, ignored or despised.

Some of these attributes we share with other beings. Animals, for example, occupy territories and have finite lives. Most animal lives end unmourned when their bones bleach in the intense desert sunshine, or decompose into the forest floor, or are eaten by prey or scavengers – or are consumed by us, with pleasure (our pleasure, that is)! Our lives, on the other hand, are part of a huge network of social relations, and at least some of these relations are profoundly changed by our death. Unlike animals, we can think, we can construct mental models of what is going on around us; we can use these models to create computer programs to help us forecast the weather; we can hold in our minds expectations about what will happen next (and look anxiously at our watches when our date hasn't turned up at the agreed time).

This, then, comprises a rough-and-ready catalogue of the properties of 'being'.

How much of this must be true of anything, including in particular 'the transcendent', in order that we might properly employ the word 'being' in relation to it? The problem is that so much of what we have said about beings – finite territory, finite life – speaks of finitude, and militates against the notion of transcendence. Linking the words 'supreme' and 'being' holds the finitude and the transcendence in some kind of balance, and for many people that will be sufficient. That we must take care to establish and sustain this balance serves as a warning against thinking of God simply as 'a being' (with the attendant implication 'just like us').

In the mid-twentieth century, some theologians, notably Rudolf Bultmann, tried to solve the problems of theology by 'de-mythologizing' the Christian faith, stripping it of myth and legend. Paul Tillich avoided this conundrum about God and being by defining God as 'the ground of our being'. God is that without which we could not be (that is to say: God is a necessary condition of our being). More recently the phrase 'Source of all being' has come into use, which sustains rather well the flavour of transcendence and origin.

'the Father almighty,'

By speaking of God now as Father we are claiming something profoundly important, namely that the experience of the transcendent is one that touches us deeply as persons – it is not just an intellectual idea to be debated and either affirmed or dismissed as nonsense.

The device by which the Jewish and Christian faiths signal this personal quality is to speak of God as Father – a very definite kind of relationship. Naturally, some people are worried by the use of a specific human relationship as the model of how we imagine God.[5] In particular, the relationship 'father of' has been so abused that for many it has entirely lost its credibility. Relationships with father are for some the stuff of enduring nightmares, not of fond memories. The 'some' may be only a minority, but their experiences must not be dismissed as irrelevant. Their stories are horribly painful to listen to, and often are retold only with great reluctance, just because they are so very painful and have left individuals traumatized for the rest of their lives. One can only listen respectfully and sensitively to such bitter experiences. In discussing the matter further, in this context, I have no desire whatsoever to brush aside such very real concerns.

Over recent decades feminist theologians have reminded us that, for our society, the father–son relationship – even at its very best – is not a truly comprehensive representation of parent–child relationships. There are dimensions of parental love that are seen only in the love of a *mother* for her children. The full range and

---

5 Sallie McFague has done us great service in her book *Models of God* (S. McFague, *Models of God: Theology for an Ecological Nuclear Age*, London, SCM Press, 1987) in which – as well as surveying the way metaphors are commonly used of God, including those mentioned here – she develops other metaphors for God: mother, lover, friend.

potential of humanness can by no means be exhausted simply by contemplating male humanness.

And let there be no recourse to that peculiarly English-language subterfuge, the use of male pronouns to include the female. In the *Los Angeles Times* of 11 October 2007 there was a piece which quoted a source from a theological seminary (which I take to be a conservative one).

> God values men and women equally, any student here will tell you that. It's just that he's given them different responsibilities in life: Men make decisions; Women make dinner.

God is not male; God is not female. We do not have in human language an appropriate pronoun for God. Even the neuter pronoun, found in some languages such as German, is inadequate for the task, for God is not a rock either. So we must be very careful indeed when our conversation about God draws in male pronouns to build arguments. In due course we may reach the point of understanding that female humanness alone is an equally defective model, but for the present we have to correct centuries of imbalance and distortion.

Even at their most positive, therefore, paternal relationships cannot now say everything that might be said about positive parenthood. The Creed was composed (like the biblical text) in a very different era, when these perspectives did not dominate the scene; it was all right to be sexist! If today we continue to rely entirely on the notion of fatherhood as representing the relationship of God to us, we run a grave risk of failing to speak in language that is understood by our contemporaries. There is an adage: how do I know what I have said until I know what you have heard? Advocates of any viewpoint or belief-system need to take note!

Nor can we overlook the fact that this view of God *as father* has shaped human self-understanding in ways that extend far beyond theology. On the one hand we have the human experience of the transcendent, and on the other a masculine model for that experience. At that level, once seen and recognized, in principle the problem is not hard to deal with, but far too often it is not seen and recognized, let alone dealt with decisively. Furthermore, in its wider ramifications this view has wrought terrible injury not only to the selfhood and the community of women, but to men and children too. God, the transcendent, has been thought of only in terms of the masculine, while other ways of thinking about God have been excluded. Therefore we have been systematically taught to deny or devalue a fundamental part of what it means to be human.

This is a huge subject about which much has been written. A full treatment lies outside the scope of this book, but if these remarks prompt reflection and wider reading, so much the better.

Somehow, we have to find a way of expressing the *general* parent–child relationship which the Creed offers as a model of the divine–human relationship, while recognizing that generalized parent–child relationships take on richness and nuance – and risk, too, let us not forget – precisely as they take the particular form of *actual* father–son, mother–daughter, father–daughter, mother–son, friend and lover relationships.

What, then, is the Creed trying to say? Surely it is that the parent–child relationship, both as a generality and in its particular forms, is one which is the embodiment of unconditional and selfless love. It is not symmetric (at least, not in the early years – or indeed in the much later years when the dependencies are often reversed as child becomes carer). It is a relationship on which – in human terms – the father sees his own future resting – or of course, the mother her own future.

In our use of the Creed, therefore, we are signalling that this 'transcendent' appears to us not only as a goal to be reached, or an aspiration to be fulfilled, but also more immediately through the same inner faculties of awareness, vulnerability and peace that we normally associate with a human relationship of complete trust and trustworthiness. This is a strong statement about humanity and human nature. What we are as persons, how we connect with one another, embodies the most important values and ideas that we could possibly know. Christian believers claim that the best context for working these ideas out is in terms of a supreme being to whom we can relate. Humanists would argue to the contrary, that if respect and care for our fellow human beings is really so important, then why don't we just get on with it? Why all this stuff about God?

We turn back, yet again, to the notion of transcendence. The humanist argument is, as I understand it, that 'humanity' is a concept that is entirely adequate to carry the weight of 'transcendence'. For many people, that is already quite sufficient to stretch the mind to breaking-point. It contends that in all our consideration of behaviour and lifestyle it is not sufficient to factor in my own interests, or those of my family, or tribe, or nation. I can no longer hide behind the claim that 'I can afford it' to justify profligate behaviour. I must bear in mind the wider good of all human beings – and there, of course, is the point of difficulty. How can I possibly cope with such an immense agenda?

But the story doesn't end there. As we are now only too well aware, to take into consideration the welfare of the human inhabitants of this planet – vast though it is – is not enough either. We are only part of a complex, delicately balanced ecosystem, and the interests of the whole transcend even the interests of the human species. Human beings need to adapt their behaviour so that the delicate balance is not upset; the penalty of failing to do so could be catastrophic for humanity as a whole – indeed, for all beings on the planet.

Fast-forward perhaps several thousand years. Assume that humanity has not (yet) caused long-term damage to the ecosystem of planet earth, and has progressed, in terms of technological accomplishment, to the point where we (or rather, our distant descendants) might seriously contemplate significant transfers of human population to nearby habitable planets. We cannot rule out the possibility that our chosen destination – indeed, the whole sector of space that embraces earth and our destination – itself forms a delicately balanced ecosystem, of whose dynamics as yet we know nothing. Yet again, in our technocratic ignorance we might perpetrate environmental damage on an even larger scale. The same considerations might apply that lead us now, in the twenty-first century, to appreciate that humanity needs to live within its means and within its environment's means. Invoking the principle of transcendence, we can at least entertain the thought that even our living companions in this neighbourhood of the Galaxy might need to be given rights requiring us to moderate our behaviour in their interests and ours.

A little historical diversion

In the first centuries of the Church, the role of the Creed was simple: it formed the basis of the profession of faith by candidates for baptism. Over the same period, however, some Christians were expressing a variant form of the Christian message. It was based upon a movement known as Gnosticism, itself a complex phenomenon which may have originated in Greece or in Persia; there were philosophical or religious movements in those parts of the world which resembled the teachings of Christian Gnostics. Its basis was a belief that the physical world is evil; in its most extreme forms, that the physical world is a delusion. The less extreme of these doctrines took the form of a claim that the evil physical world is ruled over, and even created, by Satan. This radical division of the world into spirit (good) and matter (evil) is known more generally as 'dualism'.

At first, this variation was not immediately recognized as threatening, but over time, as the idea of Satan as ruler – and particularly as creator – took shape, it became clear that here was a serious threat to the idea of God as creator and ruler over all things. Phrases were added to the Creed to make it clear to the baptismal candidates that the beliefs which they were affirming excluded the notion of multiple gods, especially that of Satan as creator of the physical world.

We have claimed that this variation was not immediately seen as a threat to the Christian community. Evidence for this is clearly available in the New Testament, when Jesus talks of the ruler of this world (John 14.30, 16.11). John was clearly not afraid of attributing this statement to Jesus.

A second reason for concern about Gnosticism emerged a little later. If, as the Gnostics maintained, all matter is evil, how could Jesus, the Word, have *become flesh*? The Gnostic solution is to claim that the Word only *appeared* to become flesh (remember '*dokein*'?); anything described in the life and death of Jesus that implied his full participation in the toils of fleshly humanity had to be expunged. So, Jesus did not die on the cross. He was spirited away and (so some claimed) Simon of Cyrene died in his place. Once again, the Church had to put down a clear marker that

Gnosticism makes nonsense of orthodox Christian teaching and must be suppressed.

A third reason for concern about Gnosticism was exposed and dealt with by Irenaeus, Bishop of Lyons, who lived from about 130 to 200 CE. The problem is this. What exactly did God create? Surely it was a good, material creation, as stated in Genesis 1. It is therefore unacceptable that it should be described in such negative terms as the Gnostics used. A supplementary question was this: was creation just the bringing of order out of chaos (implying that there was something disordered there already), or does it represent a creation from nothing? Irenaeus shifted the ground of theological and philosophical discussion by declaring that God created from nothing; the act of creation was neither limited nor required by the available resources! It was God's freely chosen act of grace.

This is a very brief summary of a long, complex and fascinating story. As a result of these tensions that surfaced over how to interpret the scriptures and how to think about God, humanity and the cosmos, the Creed took on the character of boundary-marker as well as profession of faith.

One of the things the Apostles' Creed doesn't say is: 'We believe in *one* God'. Perhaps this is because at the time no one was arguing about it, so no one needed to define the official position on this point. At various points in the Bible it is suggested that the heavenly realm is populated by many beings, but they are all creatures, subordinate to God. The worship of Yahweh (Israel's tribal God) was couched in terms such as: 'You are free to worship what you like, but don't imagine that what you are worshipping is God.'

Nevertheless, it is necessary for us to make a passing reference to this 'oneness'. This word 'one' signifies the essential unity of all things. In particular, we don't have to postulate an 'opposition', loyal or otherwise, to account for the variety of neutral or even hostile phenomena in the world we inhabit. We must simply accept things as they are and wrestle with the implications. Talk of an evil force on a par with God reveals nothing except the human desire to shift the blame onto someone else. This error is called 'dualism', and it was one of the issues that gave rise to some tough debates in the early years of the Church. In various guises it rears its head today, in worldviews in which some person, community or culture is seen as the enemy, steeped in unmitigated evil. The obvious example today is the way in which al-Qaeda and the United States regard each other. Thirty years ago the same might have been said of the mutual distrust between the USA and the USSR. Eighty years ago the Nazi regime in Germany tried to propagate a similar view of Jews. Even in the UK today there are folk who find it convenient to heap blame on 'immigrants', and see no good whatsoever in their being here.

What this belief (in the unity of all things) means, in terms of the lives of ordinary people, is that the tribulations that we humans suffer are not the consequence of being caught in the crossfire of some supernatural war whose outcome is undecided. Undoubtedly there *is* conflict, and there *is* crossfire in which we may get caught, but these take place squarely in the human world. Believers would hold that such human conflict arises and persists because we don't pay enough attention to our relationship to 'God' (or 'the transcendent', or 'the holy' or 'the sacred'). Lurking within the discussion about transcendence, and thought-experiments about space travel and wider ecologies, there might be arguments that remind us about the place of humanity in the wider context of 'life'. How big does 'big' have to be to transcend everything?

It may seem that to affirm the oneness of all things presents yet another insuperable problem: if this transcendent is responsible both for good things and for nasty things, how can we point to him (it?) as our moral compass? If God is the source of all things, both good and bad, then surely God is morally neutral – like a mountain. And for some, this raises profound questions about the idea of God. As the poet Shelley wrote:

> If he is infinitely good, what reason should we have to fear him?
> If he is infinitely wise, why should we have doubts concerning our future?
> If he knows all, why warn him of our needs and fatigue him with our prayers?[6]

---

6 P. B. Shelley, *The Necessity of Atheism*, 1811. (This is a pamphlet published anonymously while he was a student at Oxford. It is said that Shelley sent this to the authorities in the University and was promptly sent down.)

And so on in the same vein. The problems Shelley raises have exercised the minds of theologians, and thinking believers, for centuries.

'creator of heaven and earth.'

One obvious way in which the essential unity of all things, the 'almightiness' of God, can be stated very clearly is to describe God as creator. Again, we need to be on guard against an over-literal reading of the Creed at this point. The literal reading paints a picture of God as a supreme architect, designing and crafting every minute detail of the universe, from the exploding supernova to the 'friendly bacteria' that enable us to digest our food and keep our bodily systems healthy, not forgetting the ageing cells that have forgotten how to stop dividing – cancer cells.

To think of God as the architect, the designer, the builder, conjures up an image of a God with tools in his hands, crafting some aspect of our universe. The moment we head down this road, however, we run the grave risk of thinking of God as another 'thing' – a very powerful and important thing, to be sure, but nevertheless a thing. So, we must be very careful and remember that language like this is metaphorical or symbolic; we use it because we must, because it is the best we have, not because it captures in full everything that we want to say.

The history of the Church has long resounded to arguments in favour of the claim that God is creator. These always involve long words and complex ideas. They include:

1 The ontological argument: we can conceive of God, therefore God must exist.
2 The cosmological argument: the universe could not have happened spontaneously; something must have caused it.
3 The teleological argument: we see around us a trustworthy and ordered universe; something must have caused the universe to exist in this form, governed by these laws of physics rather than possible alternatives which would not favour life; there must have been a designer to plan the universe in this way.
4 The moral argument: we have a sense of right and wrong, and

> this too must have a cause. Supporters of this line of argument claim that moral notions are objective commands, and that therefore there must be a commander.

On the whole, these arguments have been found wanting *as proofs*; they may serve to bolster the confidence of believers but do not in general persuade unbelievers to believe. Underlying many of them there is a hint of a belief-system known as deism. A deist believes in God, but theirs is not the God of Christian (or for that matter Jewish or Muslim) believing. A deist's God may be an ingenious creator, but once the task of creation is over, the deist God shows no further interest in his creation or in his creatures, including us. Such a God has been described as one who sets a clockwork toy boat in motion across a pond, then loses all interest in it as it dwindles to a distant speck. Absent is any sense that we humans are being addressed, any sense that how we live actually matters, any sense that *we* matter at all. This obsessive interest in creation, the kick-starting of the universe, therefore seems a little perverse if it doesn't connect with the ongoing life of the universe.

Tina Beattie (see p. 25) ends her book by exploring this topic in some depth. Her argument may be summed up in her own words:

> When we talk about God's creation, we need to understand ourselves as characters in a work of creative genius rather than as a unique kind of godlike being in an intelligently designed universe. Design seeks to eliminate risk, because it is concerned with efficiency, function and purpose. Creativity is measured by the risk it is willing to take, for the greater the creative endeavour the greater the risk of failure.[7]

Perhaps we Christians have allowed ourselves to be drawn too far into rationalist territory, seeing God as the once-upon-a-time designer and creator and ourselves as the machine-minders. Better, says Beattie, to see God as eternally creative, and ourselves as invited to share in that creativity.

---

7 T. Beattie, *The New Atheists: The Twilight of Reason and the War on Religion*, Maryknoll, New York, Orbis Books, 2008, p. 168.

Once more, however, our focus phrase contains another element: 'heaven and earth'. What does this mean? How does it shed light on our reading of the Creed?

Let us go back, for a moment, to the previous section: the Father almighty. There we found that, in order to express one idea – the supreme-ness of God – we chose to employ rather graphic language about God's ability physically to do anything God chose. (Why *physically*? Because we have very limited imaginations: what else, other than physical activity, might be involved in *doing something*?) One possible meaning of the idea of God as creator is as an expression of that supreme-ness.

The phrase 'heaven and earth' reminds us that in Christian belief, God is responsible for *both* heaven and earth. It is a sharp rebuff to those who claimed that the physical, material world is an evil delusion created by Satan. But what are they – heaven and earth – anyway? One answer might be to go back to the very beginning of the Creed – 'I believe in God' – and remind ourselves yet again of that notion of the transcendent or the sacred. Whether it's a mental state (like thinking or dreaming) or something 'real' (like a particularly delicious apple pie), this state of exaltation and heightened awareness, the buzz from some risky but successful venture – this transcendence – is, in essence, 'where God is coming from', where God is. We might almost say that God is on a perpetual 'high'. Insofar as God has, somehow, enabled us to share in that 'high', we may say that God has created for us the possibility of heaven, and of course, the possibilities of earth – all the riches of our earthly existence.

So, *God created heaven and earth* suggests that God made possible for us this awareness of transcendence as well as the normal circumstances of daily life – not forgetting the very distinction between 'heaven' and 'earth'. That is in itself not to be dismissed as trivial; it constitutes a most important aspect of our human being, that we live not only as organisms dependent upon a physical environment (the earthly), but also as persons capable of revelling in moments of transcendence, persons who may even feel deprived without such transcendent experiences of the heavenly.

One word of warning: we must not equate God with the *experience* of transcendence, the *possibility* of transcendent experiences, or even with the *abstract idea of transcendence*. To do that transforms metaphor into illusion. God is that which makes itself known in experiences of transcendence, as well as through the joys, struggles and triumphs of earthly being.

Why all this stuff about God?

Earlier, when dealing with 'the Father almighty', we postponed a wider discussion on the question: Why introduce the God idea at all? Having identified (for example) the well-being of one's fellow humans as a legitimate goal, why not just get on with it?

It is sometimes claimed that this is a postmodernist position, on the grounds that it appears to exclude the possibility of an overarching divine guide for our actions. This, however, is not the case. The postmodernist will have to point to a concept like 'shared values' to justify any argument that his contemporaries ought (or ought not) to behave in a certain way – for example, in his wish to deter them from harming him. In other words, he cannot entirely exclude the transcendent from his thinking.

So let us look once again at that familiar word 'transcendence'. Around each one of us we may draw a circle defining a zone of particular interest. The innermost circle includes our immediate family. Successive concentric circles embrace our closest friends, our wider family, our 'kith and kin' (our tribe), our nation, our ethnic group and our species.[8]

While 'transcendence' can be defined formally, as we have done, so as to suggest that 'the transcendent' transcends all humanity (this is what believers call God), it is very easy to engage in a sort of semantic drift by which its meaning becomes rather narrower. My family's interests transcend my own, but not those of my neighbours. Such a concentric analysis of loyalties, allegiances and obligations will shape our social ethics in a way that, given

8 Perhaps it is better to suggest simply that these labels may be attached to concentric zones, without implying any particular order. For example, the ethnic group 'Slav' includes people of several nations, and commands a strong collective interest, as in the Balkan wars of the 1990s. Consider also the contrast of loyalties implied in the phrases 'English-speaking', 'Anglo-Saxon' and 'European'.

a choice or pressure of circumstances, may favour those in the smaller circle rather than the larger. By introducing the God idea, and by having God transcend every other consideration, at the very least we remind ourselves of the widest imaginable context for our ethical thought and conduct.

Of course the secular humanist can assert, and perhaps with justified indignation, that this is exactly the position he takes, and he requires no God to induce or coerce him to do so. But in his attempt to propagate his (and our) enlightened view of humanity, he will come across people (including some people of faith, sad to say) who are not persuaded. On what basis will he challenge such a partial view? Only, I suspect, by employing (albeit in a different form) precisely the concept he would deny to the believer.

Transcendence has even wider implications. It is not simply the unattainable to which we strive; it is also a boundary-marker on our human autonomy. No matter how powerful we may be in terms of human society, we are all accountable. The Old Testament scholar Walter Brueggemann put this very clearly when describing a verse in the prophecy of Isaiah challenging the great empire of Babylon: 'The self-deception of the mighty, prosperous empire is to imagine autonomy without accountability to anyone for anything.'[9] This idea pervades the entire biblical tradition. It finds expression, for example, in the Song of Mary, known as *The Magnificat*.[10]

---

9 W. Brueggemann, *Isaiah*, Louisville, Kentucky, Westminster John Knox Press, 1998, p. 98.

10 Luke 1.46–55.

6

Jesus

It is all very well to have the elaborate notions of transcendence, lofty ideals or high hopes. Somehow they have to be earthed, rooted in human experience in a way that makes them accessible, yet without blunting the edge of that word 'transcendence'. In the Christian faith this need is met in the person of Jesus Christ.

Faith in Christ is centred on an event known to Christians as the incarnation, in which God is said to have become man. We shall of course come to consider in some detail the interpretation of this event in which God is described as identifying Godself with fallen and suffering humanity. It is also possible – and there is ample support for this view in the New Testament – that the intended outcome of the incarnation is that human persons should be able to identify with Jesus and in some sense become like him, come to share his nature. In other words, the identification can be two-way: as God identifies with us in Christ, so we can identify ourselves with God in Christ. Our presentation of this central section of the Creed dealing with Jesus Christ is set out in a manner which I hope exposes the possibilities of working with this story in a mythic or symbolic way – remembering, of course, that myth is not under any circumstances to be equated simplistically with falsehood, nor does it exclude other ways of reading the story.

I have chosen to cluster the clauses of the Creed which deal with Jesus into four groups, concerned with identity, story, meaning and destiny. The 'ultimate questions' that people ask about themselves cluster around these same four words. Who am I? What is the story (better, what are the stories) of which my life is part? What does it all mean? What will it all add up to in the end? By presenting this material in this way, I hope it will be possible for more people to identify those questions, as they arise for them, with the same questions as they gather around the person of Jesus.

Identity

At this point the Creed focuses our attention upon the identity of a particular person in a particular historical and cultural context. (I refer here to 'this person', not to be coy about the gender of the person, as if I had something sinister to hide, but precisely to make the point that gender is not central to our thinking about this person.) In due course, perhaps inevitably and perhaps not, we shall use less evasive language about this person, but remember: a marker has been put down.

We are drawn into a number of questions: Who is this person? What do I know about this person? Why is this person special? Who can identify with this person? Can I identify with this person? What does this person's story tell me about my own identity? Am I able to follow this person's life-journey, and from that experience draw wisdom and strength?

'I believe in Jesus Christ,'

Some versions of the Apostles' Creed begin this section rather differently: 'And in Jesus Christ'. Harned[1] makes great play of this apparently trivial variation. For him, the word 'and' both unites the Father and the Son, and at the same time distinguishes them one from the other. The speaker, therefore, cannot profess belief in the Father without in the same sentence professing belief in the Son.

There are four components here: Jesus, Christ, believe, and I.

Jesus is an historical figure, born in Judaea about 6 or 7 BCE (Before the Common Era – the commonly accepted scheme of dating, worldwide). Little is known with certainty about the cir-

1 D. B. Harned, *Creed and Personal Identity: The Meaning of the Apostles' Creed*, Philadelphia, Fortress Press, 1981.

cumstances of his birth, or about his early life. At some point – perhaps in his early thirties – he emerged as a travelling preacher and (so it is said) healer. For some reason he touched raw nerves among the religious and political establishment, and was put to death.

This 'disaster' left his disciples initially traumatized and confused. But various events over the following few weeks gave rise to a personal inner transformation, as a result of which this small (but growing) group of disciples concluded that Jesus was not merely a charismatic preacher: somehow his life reflected the life of God in an unprecedented and unique way. In his own human person he embodied the transcendent God. When, later, they began to tell stories about the life of Jesus, they were not shy of admitting their own stupidity in failing to see him in this way, even though they did remember some fleeting moments of recognition.

The story of Jesus is of course set in an historical context. His contemporaries believed certain things. Certain ideas would have outraged them, not least the idea that the transcendent God could somehow be squeezed into the dimensions of human life.

Within their own culture, the way which the disciples of Jesus found to be the clearest expression of this mould-breaking awareness was to describe Jesus as Messiah (Aramaic) or Christ (Greek) – both words conveying the sense of a human person specially chosen by God to deliver his people from oppression. The term 'Messiah' was not precisely defined in Jewish thought, but in the context of Roman occupation it was only to be expected that this figure would prompt hopes of a military deliverer. In fact Jesus offered a drastic re-interpretation of Messiahship, so although the Messiah concept was the basis of Christian thinking about Jesus, it underwent significant transformation. The word 'Christ', on the other hand, conveyed a notion of a divinely appointed and anointed *representative of God*. Here too a good deal of re-interpretation was going on; Jesus wasn't going to fit snugly into any already existing human category. This story required – to put it bluntly – a lot of careful selling to the contemporary Jewish audience, and the way to do so was to point out that the ideas that Jesus embodied emerged quite naturally from their own religious tradition – in fact, from the Old Testament prophets. This procedure is entirely characteristic of the biblical tradition, which is why we spent some time, earlier, in getting to grips with biblical language.

In short, then, they came to 'believe in him'. To 'believe in' something is a phrase we often use without really thinking what we mean. Sometimes our intention is to express acceptance of a proposition such as 'France lies across the Channel'. Often we use the phrase to indicate a kind of commitment to, or faith in, some principle: 'I believe in having a good breakfast to set you up for the day' or 'I don't believe in capital punishment'. In the case of that little company of the friends of Jesus – and all those who twenty centuries later make the same claim – to believe in Jesus means to trust him, to make a lifetime commitment to him as a person (that is, to follow as closely as possible his way of doing things), and to accept the insights into the nature of God that he presented in his life and teaching.

So, 'I believe in Jesus Christ' is very far from simply agreeing with a statement such as 'The moon is made of green cheese'. A key word is 'I'; it is a belief that emerges from (or reaches into) the very depths of our being, in a way that mere assent to a proposition could never do. It expresses something of our sense of who we are, and why we tick. This 'I believe' is the same as the initial 'I believe' with which the Apostles' Creed began.

'God's only Son, our Lord,'

The idea that Jesus in some way 'embodied the transcendent' (a far-from-perfect phrase) grew over a period of about five centuries, through debate, argument, and even persecution of one group within the Church by another. It is possible to trace, even within the New Testament (a first-century product) some evidence that this idea evolved over time.

When the early Church hit upon the phrase 'Son of God', however, they weren't inventing a new idea; they were again borrowing from their cultural past as Jews and as folk of what we now call the Middle East. A son – particularly the eldest son – was a highly significant member of a family. He bore his father's *likeness* (we now know this to be genetically rooted, of course); he inherited his father's *qualities*; he inherited his father's *authority*; and he inherited his father's *estate*. Centuries before Jesus, these attributes were associated with the person of the king, who is referred to in several psalms as 'Son of God'. So, in one sense, its application to Jesus is not quite as startling as one might suppose. But the word 'only' in this clause is highly significant, claiming for Jesus a unique status.

What exactly do we mean, then, by believing that Jesus was the Son of God? In Jesus' time and before, the father–son relationship, as we have seen, implies that the father and the son are at one in the ownership and disposition of the family assets. There is between them a trust that is deep and enduring.

If 'Jesus was/is the Son of God (= God)' is a metaphorical statement, are we, in believing, simply assenting to the statement as metaphor, or are we assenting to its literal truth?

Suppose that we insist on taking it literally according to our twenty-first century understanding of the words 'father' and 'son'. What would follow from that? First of all there are huge questions. The human relationship 'father of' is defined in two ways: genesis and nurture, passing on of genes and passing on of values. We have spoken above of likeness, qualities, authority and estate. In biblical times it was these attributes that were linked with the idea of paternity and sonship, not with DNA. I know of no one who has claimed, as the implication of this phrase of the Creed, that if it were possible to take a DNA sample from Jesus (which, because he lived as a real man, should in principle have been possible, though quite beyond our reach now) then we should be able to identify God's genetic makeup.

On the other hand, if we focus this claim upon values rather than genetics, then three things follow. First, the claim that Jesus is God's Son moves abruptly from the absurd to the plausible. In ancient Jewish culture, the king was God's chosen and designated representative and was referred to as God's Son, the bearer of God's values and guardian of God's people. Second, the question of Virgin Birth (see below under 'he was conceived by the Holy Spirit') also changes in character. There is no need to ask, 'If we are agreed that the male contribution to Jesus' DNA could not have been God's, then whose was it?' Third, there may be no need to be concerned with the distinction between a literal and a non-literal reading of this clause of the Creed.

In a sense it may be easier for us than it was for the first Christians to believe that Jesus is appropriately described as Son of God, because no one alive now has fully shared their experience, from the point of view either of their cultural presuppositions about God or of their encounters with the living Jesus. There are many who have experienced something akin to it, within the limitations of time and space, but the actual experience of the twelve? – no one. It is easier (at least I think so) for us now to believe that a human person whose dated life took place 2,000 years ago represents God to us perfectly, rather than someone whom we might approach, hear his (or of course her) voice, accent, mannerisms, imperfections (did he eat with his mouth open?). *In that sense* Jesus is a fantasy;[2] there is nothing we know about him that might cause us to dislike him as a human being. There is nothing about his humanness that might repel us or even attract us, though what we do know about him suggests that he had a very considerable impact on his contemporaries. We see him, therefore, in part as a particular human being (about whom we know very little, and virtually nothing of the normal stuff of friendship), and in part as a special type of human being – one who represents to us the transcendent, the presence of the sacred, the unattainable possibilities for which nevertheless we feel impelled to strive.

In the first decades of the Church's existence, the confession 'Jesus is Lord' was the sum total of its creed. This term 'Lord' signified a relationship involving allegiance and obedience, as well as protection and defence. It was clearly a threat to the total commitment of the Roman citizen (or citizen of a client state) to the emperor. So it was also the signal for persecution, even execution, of the confessing Christian. In those far-off days, to confess Jesus as Lord was not a way of saying, 'I'm a nice respectable sort of person'; rather, it was a death warrant with your own signature on it.

We are reminded here of David Harned's description[3] of the

2 I am very conscious that to use these words risks offending some readers. But please note the qualifying phrase, 'in that sense'.

3 Harned, *Creed and Personal Identity*, p. 19.

Creed as 'identity avowal' – not merely a profession of belonging, but an assertion that we find our identity entirely and exclusively in this affirmation.

'he was conceived by the Holy Spirit,'

This clause of the Creed introduces another idea, but for its full affirmation we must wait a little. Here the emphasis is still on Jesus.

From what we've said already, we are clear that in the terms of the Creed, Jesus was – and is – a very special, indeed a unique, person. But what is it that marks him out as special? In what way was he unique? It's not just a matter of how he lived his life – his 'style'; it's also a matter of *who* he was (and is). In other words, his conduct, what he did and the way he did it, is of a piece with the person he was. You can't have one without the other. Who, then, was he?[4]

Where better to begin than with his origins? Here, yet again, we need to remember our discussion on biblical language. If the biblical writers wanted to say something, they had to employ the right words and the appropriate word-pictures to convey that meaning to another person steeped in their tradition. From a distance of two or more millennia we may find those word-pictures unhelpful, but that does not mean we can abandon the attempt to grasp their underlying meaning. In what follows we shall make exactly that attempt, in the hope of discerning the underlying meaning while not destroying the word-pictures which have, for most people, even yet, a capacity to evoke a sense of the sacred.

In the mid-twentieth century a debate raged about the relative importance of nature and nurture, whether birth (breeding) or upbringing was more influential in determining an individual's character. Clearly, in Jesus' time nature was held to play a key role. We can see this from the importance of questions about his birthplace, and from various debates in which Jesus became involved during his preaching career. For the later Church it wasn't enough simply to claim that he was a good man, or even a charismatic

4 It is important to Christians that in some sense Jesus is still with us. It isn't appropriate to pick up this theme right now. I do try to address it later.

preacher; yet to claim any more than that was deeply offensive to many of their influential contemporaries.

So, the way in which the Christian faith has always expressed all this has been to begin at the beginning. The claim that Jesus was like no other man is, on this view, best substantiated by claiming that *at the very moment of his conception* he was like no other man. Clearly, that immediately limits the influence of the 'nurture' side of the argument, because his conception necessarily precedes any nurture. Nurture by parents may give the individual foetus and the child the best possible chance, or may blight its development; nurture cannot replace or re-engineer the original genetic endowment (although of course the continuing development of gene therapies may soon make that possibility a matter of routine). With our modern knowledge we are aware that what a mother does during pregnancy has consequences for the baby's well-being in later life; but the moment of conception, surely, stands out as the *starting-point of the process* by which the baby's uniqueness is given its particular shape.

In this clause of the Apostles' Creed we find one of the most mind-stretching claims of all: that somehow, at the moment of Jesus' conception, the normal processes of human origin were simultaneously *both* running their normal course *and* being overridden by the direct influence of God. We may wonder why, as a consequence, the role of a human father was marginalized. But that is not the point. Nor are we being invited to ponder, or sneer at, the idea of supernatural conception. We are not talking here about scientific impossibilities. We are talking about meaning. Somehow (in ways that are quite beyond the reach of human language) in Jesus the heart of God entered human life *right at the very beginning*. From then on, everything was utterly normal.

Incidentally, it is interesting to reflect on this in the context of current debates about the moment when a foetus acquires the rights of a human person. Many Christians would argue that this takes place at the moment of conception. Could there be a link between this ethical belief (which is one of the points of difference between conservative Christians on the one hand, and Muslims on the other) and the insistence of the New Testament on the role of the Holy Spirit in Jesus' conception?

The stories of the birth of Jesus are really rather odd. On the one hand the prophets hinted strongly that the Messiah would be a lineal descendant of the great King David. So Joseph was proclaimed to be 'of the house and lineage of David'. Fine! But then apparently the Gospels go on to declare that in terms of his DNA, Jesus owed nothing whatever to Joseph! Now, we can of course argue that, however smart St Luke was as a doctor, he knew nothing at all about DNA. That knowledge didn't come our way for another nineteen-and-a-half centuries! On the other hand, we have no difficulty in believing that in a patriarchal society such as first-century Palestine they knew what was important about paternity.

We believe, then, that Jesus was 'conceived by the Holy Spirit'. Whatever we choose to believe about Jesus' DNA, we hold on to this: his birth was an act of God (i.e. it reflected the transcendent) in a sense matched by no other human birth. It is a commonplace for new parents, particularly Christian parents, to express the belief that a new-born child is a gift from God; that the birth of the child is a miracle of grace, and so on. All of that was true of Jesus too. But by declaring that he was conceived by the Holy Spirit, we are expressing our conviction that in Jesus, God acted in a totally unique way.

Yet there's a trap here, because if in his birth Jesus totally sidesteps the normal laws of cause and effect, then he isn't really human at all, and can't identify with our human condition. He can be the bearer of transcendence, certainly, but not in the momentous way that Christians attribute to him. This was the view held by the community called the Gnostics. As we have seen, their origins are uncertain; it may be that they arose in Judaism, or perhaps with the Zoroastrians in Persia. In terms of their part in the Christian story, however, we need to be aware that they had great difficulties with the idea that the material world could be the handiwork of God. For this present discussion it is relevant to know that they so despised the material world that some believed that Jesus, the Son of God, could not have been part of it. This phrase in the Creed is, then, a rebuttal of that position. By affirming unequivocally that Jesus was conceived, we implicitly deny the truth of this particular branch of Gnosticism.

So, our Creed goes on to a further clause: 'born of the Virgin Mary'.

'born of the Virgin Mary,'

This clause endorses the claims of the previous clause that the ultimate origins of the human Jesus lie outside the human sphere and that from then on the life of Jesus emerged into the world perfectly normally. It also breaks new ground, however, by declaring that central to the whole story is the willingness of a young peasant woman to be available to God for this amazing purpose. If Luke the doctor were writing now, would he be using terms like 'informed consent'? Certainly, the Creed is here making a profound statement about human life, for Mary's role is not merely that of an 'extra', recruited for a walk-on part with no 'lines' to say beyond 'be it unto me according to thy word'. Her *willingness* is essential to the story. This suggests that close to the heart of the deep meaning contained in the Creed is the idea that, while God has his purposes for us, it is not in the divine nature to dictate or impose. To the observant reader of the Old Testament, this may come as something of a surprise, for the Old Testament contains many stories that suggest God is indeed coercive.

Here, then, is an idea that the Church has held to be important enough to be enshrined in one of its key foundational texts. However overwhelming the forces of nature and the momentum of history may seem to be, there is an area of individual human responsibility which will be respected by God, if not always by our fellow humans.

We turn now to the second key word in this clause: 'Virgin'.

Words are slippery things. We like to think they are exact, that they can grapple with a meaning and hold it down for good and all. But they can't, because the meanings change even as the words are trying to hold them down. Even creeds are built on these slippery things. Compiling a creed must have been like holding an eel. No sooner have you got one end securely in place than the other end develops a mind of its own and escapes from your control. Over the centuries the changes have been enormous, and profoundly alter the meaning of what is being said.

Let me give you an example: the word 'indifferent'. Today we use it to mean that a person really doesn't care one way or another. She's got better things to do. A couple of hundred years ago it would have meant something rather different, more like: impartial, not taking sides, unprejudiced. How would you react to a judge who 'indifferently ministered justice'? You might take the view that he was not paying proper attention to his job; he was doing it without caring. A sporting journalist reporting on a cricket match may describe the fielding as 'indifferent', and we'd have no difficulty in decoding that as a thinly veiled criticism! The meaning of the word has changed.

How about 'Virgin'? Here, we have to look back rather further. Until about the third century, this word simply meant 'young woman of marriageable age'. It didn't mean 'sexually innocent' or anything like it.

It was in that sense that the prophet Isaiah was using the word when he wrote of his encounter with Ahaz, the king.[5] They were talking about a grave military threat to their country from two neighbouring states. The population was on iron rations, to try to ensure that the food supplies lasted as long as possible. Isaiah (a senior civil servant) was trying to say to Ahaz something like this: 'Don't worry, my dear fellow. Before you know what's happening, those two kings that you dread will be dead and gone, and their kingdoms in ruins.' This was how he made his point: 'Here's a young woman. She's going to have a child. By the time the child is on solids, he will be eating curds and honey.' (This was a delicacy undreamed of during the siege.) 'By the time this child is old enough to know the difference between right and wrong, those enemies of yours will be consigned to the dustbin of history.'

That's roughly what Isaiah said. From the Hebrew, the translation 'young woman' is entirely accurate. But then the book of Isaiah was translated into Greek, along with the rest of the Old Testament. And the Greek word chosen to correspond with the Hebrew 'young woman' was one that certainly meant 'a young woman who has had no sexual experience'. Quite how this slip-up happened we don't really know. But it has cast a long shadow!

---

5 See Isaiah 7, especially vv. 14–16.

And that, in part, was how the idea of a virgin birth came to be: Isaiah's little tale about a conversation with his royal master came to be used as a prophecy about Jesus.

Of course, that was only one line that led to the idea of the virgin birth. More strictly, we ought to refer to the *virginal conception* of Jesus.

So here the concern is quite the opposite. Having ensured that Jesus is clearly 'out of the ordinary' (i.e. divine), the compilers of the Creed were desperate to make it equally clear that Jesus is 'truly human'. So, for all his 'specialness' he had to be born, just like everyone else. He didn't simply appear on the stage of human history like a character in a play; he was born into poverty and insecurity; he shared our human limitations. This, of course, is what had so upset the Christian Gnostics and the Arians; for them, the idea of Jesus the Son of God actually sharing human limitations was quite unacceptable.

In handling this aspect of our belief in this way, the Creed seems to me to be trying to pre-empt the question: 'OK, so Jesus is both human and divine; how exactly did this happen?' And their answer is simple: 'Jesus' mother had not yet had sex with any man, let alone Joseph her betrothed; Jesus' conception was miraculous and attributable only to divine intervention. Once you've got that into your head, everything else fits into place.' This is the perspective of Matthew and Luke, the authors of two of the New Testament Gospels. Their stories about the birth of Jesus are offered as an attempt to explain the inexplicable

John and Mark, the other two Gospel-writers, take quite a different approach. They simply say (so it seems to me): 'Don't worry about explanations; you'll do your head in before you come up with a satisfactory answer. Just take it from me that you have to accept that Jesus was both human and divine. Don't argue; just accept it. Why do we say so? Because it's the only way we can deal with our experience of Jesus.'

So, Matthew's and Luke's stories: brilliant tales of Jesus' origins. John's and Mark's approach: there it is, a fact of *our* experience that can be a fact of *your* experience, take it or leave it. Before he describes any action, Mark declares boldly: 'The beginning of the Good News of Jesus Christ, the Son of God.' I take him to be saying something like this: 'I'm going to set out in this Gospel the story of Jesus Christ the Son of God. Watch his disciples as they flounder and fumble, never getting the message. Watch as a Gentile Roman soldier is the first to recognize the truth.'

Perhaps John put it best when he wrote: 'He who has seen me has seen the father.' My reading of these words goes like this: 'When you see Jesus, you see God – or, at least, you get the best insight your brain can handle into what God is like. And you get nothing else. So, that's why we believe Jesus is God.'

I do have a problem with this clause in the Creed. I certainly believe what it is trying to express, but I have a real problem with the way it is trying to express it. If you don't have such a problem, then I hope that by reading this you may come to understand why other people do; while if you share my difficulty, I hope you will be encouraged to believe that even as you struggle, you can nevertheless be very much part of the community of faith.

We come back to the nub of the whole problem – literal or metaphorical? I can see a line of argument that says it's all far too insecure unless you go for 'literal'; with 'metaphorical' or 'symbolic' you don't know where you are. But in my view there are grave drawbacks with 'literal'. And this is my whole point; what has motivated me in attempting this project is to argue that 'only the literal explanation is acceptable under any circumstances' is for many people untenable, while 'these statements may have a metaphorical interpretation' is intellectually and emotionally satisfying, and leaves entirely open the quest for truth.

Having said that, I have to admit that there is a possible danger in going down the route of continuing a quest for truth. Many people have gone down that road and kept their minds perpetually open. They never commit themselves to anything, and so never grasp for themselves the possibilities of faith. On that view, one may ask such a person: if the quest is really worthwhile, why does it never end?

But I believe that is not the alternative. Earlier in this book we heard the words of St Anselm about faith seeking understanding. Something is going on in our hearts (faith) which on rational grounds is baffled and bemused, but continues to look for a way of rooting itself in understanding.

To put it rather sharply, the literal approach (for me) pictures the seeking human as knocking on a big door, under his arm a bundle of papers with his questions written on them. Eventually God opens the door and shoves into his hand another bundle of papers with the answers written on them. 'There you are, there are your answers, work it all out for yourself.'

The metaphorical approach, in contrast, begins in the same way, but this time God opens the door and invites the seeking human in for a conversation.

The Creed talks in terms of a kind of logic. In this clause the Creed is saying, as it often does, that the important test is to get the belief in your head right and everything will follow. Mark and John are saying, 'Accept the experience of Jesus as we, the first disciples, knew him, and you will come as we have done to believe this about Jesus.'

Story

We all have a story. From our birth to our death it will be marked by twists and turns, ups and downs, hopes and disappointments, achievements and failures. Moreover, our story will be linked to other stories, of our parents and grandparents and those of the people who are closest to us. Again questions come crowding in: Why did he do that, all those years ago? What on earth did she see in him? Am I seeing a pattern here, across the generations, in the ways of parents with their children, husbands with their wives?

Again, as we reflect upon the story of Jesus – not simply reading about it but reflecting upon it – we may want to ask other questions: Is this life, with its own ups and downs, misunderstandings and harsh cruelties, a life that offers a vantage-point from which to evaluate the miseries and joys of the world I live in? Am I able to follow this person's life-journey, and from that experience draw wisdom and strength for my own?

'suffered under Pontius Pilate,'

One of the oddest things about the Creed is the way it fast-forwards from Jesus' birth to his death. Is his death, in fact, the only other thing we need to know about him? What was it about his life – the time he shared with that little band of followers – that led them to take the stand they later did in respect of Jesus and his message? There must have been *something* striking about him as their travelling companion; the manner of his death couldn't surely have been the entire story? After all, the four Gospel-writers had access to records (which may have been oral) about what Jesus said and did during the three or so years of his public activity, and they felt this was important material. Why does the Creed say nothing about all this?

In a sense it does, by implication. As we shall see, there had to be an explanation for his execution (for that was what it was). In opening up that question we shall discover something about the public activity of Jesus. For now, however, let us stick with the Creed itself.

We have already touched on the reasons behind the death of Jesus (see above). It is important to the Church that its faith is rooted in history. It is not *purely* myth, although, given the part played by metaphor in Christian theology, some degree of myth inevitably surrounds that history. The appearance of Pilate (the only person to be named in the Creed, apart from Jesus himself and Mary) meets that need for historical grounding. Pilate was, quite definitely, Roman governor of the Province of Judaea from 26 to 37 CE. As such, he exercised immense power, in which his objectives were to defend the interests of the Roman Empire, and to ensure that the Roman elite took a considerable profit from his patronage and (to use today's word) corruption.

Pilate was not, therefore, the weak stooge of the Jerusalem establishment. *His* writ ran, and no one else's. He decided to execute Jesus because it was in Rome's interest that he should. The possibility of insurrection could not be tolerated, so Jesus had to die – even though Pilate was far from convinced of his judicial guilt. To that extent, then, Pilate's authority was not entirely autonomous; he was required by his Roman masters to respond to the circumstances he found in his particular province. If those circumstances called for heavy-handedness, or shrewd – even devious – negotiation, then so be it.

The first century or so of the Church's story are marked by an interesting theme. In the Gospel accounts of the death of Jesus it is clear that *both Pilate and the Jewish authorities are complicit in his conviction*, though only the Romans had the authority to determine and carry out the death sentence. From that point on, the way in which that story was told required great delicacy; its authors had to negotiate a veritable minefield in order to allay Roman suspicion. One of these factors was the truth – that, as set out above, Pilate alone carried responsibility for the death sentence, albeit under considerable pressure from the Jewish authorities who, if they chose, could create public order problems at the drop of a hat. There may have been an element of bluff here; the Jewish authorities would have no difficulty in seeing that to create public-order problems would result in ruthless repression by Pilate, which would risk everything they had toiled so hard to preserve.

The other factor, however, arose rather later, when Christianity was beginning to spread across the Empire and its reputation had taken a subversive shape. In 69 CE, after a power struggle in Rome, Vespasian became Emperor. To confirm his own legitimacy he ordered his son Titus to destroy the nascent Jewish state in Palestine, no matter what it cost, simply as a warning signal to anyone inclined to dispute his own rule. After a bitter and brutal siege, Jerusalem was destroyed and the temple razed to the ground. From that point on, it was a matter of high politics how the Christian movement positioned itself in relation to the Jewish community. Furthermore, the imperial authorities would not take kindly to a sect whose very founder was executed by the decree of a Roman governor. That would mean either that Jesus was a criminal (his sect would immediately be discredited, and his followers would carry that criminal taint for ever), or that he was innocent, and anyone attributing his execution to Roman influence would be guilty of subversion. So, in many of the key texts, blame for the death of Jesus is laid at the door not of the governor but of the chief priest and his circle.[6] By the time this really became an issue for the Church, the temple was in ruins, so no harm would be done by shading the story in such a way as to impute blame to Jerusalem rather than Rome.

By the time the formulation in the Apostles' Creed was agreed, Rome itself had changed beyond recognition; indeed, the wheels were beginning to come off the chariot that was the Roman Empire. The Christian faith was establishing itself very firmly at the heart of civilization, having outgrown its Jewish roots. Attributing blame for the death of Jesus, therefore, was no longer the delicate matter it had once been. The degree of 'economy with the truth' involved in blaming the Jews for Jesus' death has, however, left its own dreadful legacy: anti-Semitism.

We have already referred to another reason for the emphasis on the suffering and death of Jesus: the belief among Christians sympathetic to the Gnostic movement that it was inconceivable for Jesus to be so fully engaged with material, physical humanity as to experience pain, suffering and death. Such a level of identification was, however, essential to the Christian gospel. To a people who were themselves suffering persecution, a Jesus who by adroit footwork neatly evaded pain and suffering would have had no credibility as a role-model, let alone as a Saviour.

'was crucified, died, and was buried;'

Here we're still firmly in the arena of history. The fact of Jesus' death and the manner of Jesus' death are included here in a central statement of the Christian faith. 'He was crucified' reiterates in different words the involvement of Rome in his execution. Only a Roman squad could have carried out such an execution.

But there is more. Crucifixion was the means by which the local population was kept under the heel of the Roman legions. It was calculated to inflict the maximum pain and humiliation on the victim and, by association, on the cause, whatever it might be, that the victim represented. By elevating this comparatively trivial historic fact into an article of a creed, the Church is underlining

6 See, for example, Acts 2.23, 7.52 etc.

the way Jesus identified with the most wretched of people. At his death, as well as at his birth, Jesus was just an ordinary person. And this, of course, leaves us all with a real puzzle. How can 'an ordinary person' come to be thought of as the perfect reflection of the transcendent (or whatever form of words you prefer to capture your understanding of 'God')? What does this mean, if anything, for the rest of us 'ordinary people'?

Following the death of Jesus, it is alleged, attempts were made by the authorities to ensure that his memory faded rapidly from the public mind. There were theories that he did not in fact die but was brought down from the cross alive and quietly spirited away to live out his days in safe obscurity, a solution that would certainly have suited the Gnostics. It has fuelled the uproar surrounding popular fiction like *The Da Vinci Code.*[7] Like the Gospels, the Apostles' Creed is very up-front about it: this did not happen; Jesus died and was buried. These words are very explicit in denying even the faintest possibility of escape. Jesus died. His life was over. Full stop! The end!

What the death of Jesus *meant* is another matter entirely. Other creeds are explicit about *why* Jesus died (in other words, they make claims about its meaning). Here, the Apostles' Creed is content to set out the Church's claims as to the basic facts of the case. We must now, therefore, pause in our tour of the Creed to consider this matter more deeply.

Why did Jesus die?

To this question there are two kinds of answer. The first kind looks at the human story surrounding Jesus' death. In what way did he so annoy his contemporaries that, despite the good impression he had made generally, they felt they had no option but to kill him?

At the time, the country was under rather oppressive Roman occupation. The domestic political scene was very complex. The senior figures in the Jewish religious establishment were desper-

---

7 D. Brown, *The Da Vinci Code: A Novel*, London and New York, Bantam Press, 2003.

ately anxious not to irritate the Roman governor or provoke him to violent recrimination against them, their values or their culture. These people were associated with the temple in Jerusalem; their central concern was to preserve the physical institutions of temple worship – the very heart, for them, of their faith and culture.

Various other groupings were equally concerned to ensure that their religion survived intact, not merely institutionally but in terms of authentic personal piety. Some of these groupings shared the life of the whole community; it was their rather puritanical lifestyle that marked them out. Other groups in this general category were so disenchanted with ordinary society that they established communes, living far from the cities according to a very rigorous code of belief and conduct. There have been suggestions that John the Baptist, and maybe even Jesus himself, had some links with one of these communes.

Yet other groups were deeply angered by the Roman occupation; from time to time these feelings erupted in the form of insurgencies – though that is perhaps to overstate what actually happened. Most of these were quickly and brutally put down by the forces of imperial Rome, leaving almost no trace.

Jesus seems to have alienated all three groups: by his remarks about the temple; by his apparently high-handed re-working of the codes of conduct so esteemed by the second group; and by his refusal to play the rebellious games of the third group. By various devious machinations, these groups engineered Jesus' death.

The second kind of answer tries to relate the death of Jesus to our experience of being human, and our experience of God. In Christian theology this is known as 'atonement' – 'at-one-ment', the 'process' by which the renewal of our distorted relationship with the transcendent God is made possible. Throughout history there have been several different ways of interpreting or understanding atonement. In the following pages I try to summarize the main 'theories' of atonement.

Following Anselm's definition of theology as 'faith seeking understanding' – and faith *continues always* to seek understanding – we are perpetually in search of understanding; we never have it entirely in our grasp and under our control. And nowhere is this more evident than at the foot of the cross.

Earlier, when introducing the idea of a creed, we found three words that between them seemed to describe a great diversity of ways of understanding what it means to be a Christian: behaving, believing and belonging.[8] Of the alternative descriptions on offer, the way in which we can best make sense of the death of Jesus seems to be in terms of the 'behaving' model of being a Christian.

Guilt has for a long time been a powerful and dangerous word in the Christian tradition. It's perhaps understandable why the biblical tradition sets it up as the clearest description of the journey people have to make to find their place in God's family. Ethics, the way we behave towards one another, was a key feature of Old Testament religion, and of course it remains so today. God expects certain things of us in terms of our lifestyle and behaviour. If we ignore those expectations, our lives will run into trouble sooner or later. Not the least significant kind of trouble is a profound inner anxiety caused simply by guilt. The 'behaving' model captures that need very graphically. Perhaps it's time to look in a little more detail at explanations of the meaning of the cross that are of this general kind.

First, we look at the idea of sin, the complex and so easily misunderstood fault-line in our relationship with God, and the atonement theories that sprang directly from it. Then we can examine alternative theories which seem to be less hooked on guilt as the underlying cause of all problems.

What is the nature of this problem. Traditionally Christians have called it *sin* or, sometimes, *sins*. This obscures what the Christian community has really been saying. Look at Romans 1 for an analysis. What do you think Paul is saying about the nature of sin?

Some writers and preachers make a distinction between *sin*, the condition of estrangement, and *sins*, the misdirected or exclusively self-directed actions that are the consequence of sin. On this analysis, sins are the symptoms of the deeper and more serious condition, sin. And it is primarily to this deeper condition that the work of Jesus is addressed. Some have talked about being 'put

8 We shall return to them later.

right with God'. In John's Gospel, for example, the crucial failure of humanity is in not recognizing Jesus as the expression of God's values – in short, as the Son of God. This is shorthand for not recognizing God when we see God.

This condition of estrangement from God has a particular quality about it that sets it apart from other experiences of estrangement. In most such experiences, it is possible to relate present discomfort to past delights. If a human relationship has broken down, our feelings of hurt and loss arise partly from the disorienting fact of fracture, and partly from the very positive intensity of the relationship as it used to be. If the relationship was neither very intense nor very positive, the feeling of estrangement will be relatively mild (though other attendant circumstances, such as financial loss, may be just as serious). If, on the other hand, the relationship had been a very close one, the estrangement will be felt as bewildering pain. The individual experiencing this pain will be able to relate it to the supportive relationship which is now no longer.[9]

Estrangement from God, on the other hand, differs in that there may be only a faint murmur in the depths of one's being that something is wrong. There is no conscious memory of things having ever been otherwise. There is no standard by which the present condition can be evaluated or diagnosed, merely an intractable question about, for example, the meaning of it all. For some people this sense of unease is not something they feel able to reflect upon, but they can and do react to its presence. They often try to correct or compensate for the feeling that life has no meaning by acting in ways that are anti-social or in some cases criminal, damaging either to themselves or to others. These damaging acts and lifestyles are called sins.

Before we go on, we should set out the whole framework, so that we can see how Christians believe that both the condition of estrangement and its destructive symptoms are dealt with. This is where the technical language of traditional theology gets a bit 'heavy'. And before we go into it, we need to 'come clean' and

9 Sadly, some children are brought up in a way that leaves them with no sense that they were ever in an intense positive relationship (with their parents). They have known nothing but estrangement from their earliest days.

state clearly that although this account (or one like it) will make sense for many people, there will be others for whom it makes no sense at all. Other approaches are possible.

So, let's go ahead with this particular story. Though we present it as a narrative – a story with a beginning, a middle and an end – its elements may not occur in that order.

First, the person recognizes that something is wrong, which is likely to involve an experience of remorse or shame at the sins in which they have participated, perhaps an acknowledgement of the damage done to themselves and others. Sooner or later the person will come to understand the seriousness of the *underlying* condition of sin. As we have seen, however, the sense of remorse or shame following moral failure doesn't have the cutting edge it once did. For many people, the primary sensation (when it is powerful enough to be felt at all) is this sense of inner and outer disorder that Tillich called 'estrangement'.

Whatever word best describes this complex awareness, it is then possible to acknowledge the seriousness of it all, and one's personal complicity in and responsibility for it. The technical term for this is 'confession'. We must be clear, however, that what is important is not a series of words said by or to the repentant person, but rather a radical awareness of the situation.

Second, there needs to be a desire to see change, a longing for life to be different, a determination to put the past of sins behind and focus on a future in a renewed relationship with God, a relationship untainted by sin. The technical word for this resolve is 'repentance'. It looks back in sorrow and remorse, and forward in trust and hope to a future that is radically different from the past. It recognizes that I myself need to change; it's no use expecting externals to change and bring about the silencing of those painful thoughts.

Third, the person must claim the possibility of reconciliation with God that is brought about and offered by the work of Christ. (We shall need to say more later about the important distinction between 'brought about' and 'offered', but it can rest for now.) This is the crucial moment. It has various technical names: 'the new birth', or 'justification'.

Fourth, there is the ongoing process by which the sins gradually fade from view as the inclination to engage in them wanes under the influence of the Holy Spirit. This we call 'sanctification', the process whereby the new life blossoms and bears fruit in relationship with God.

These ideas have taken shape over many centuries through people's insight into the human condition and the part that the idea of God can play in clarifying and correcting what is wrong.

We can now turn to a group of theories, perhaps the earliest of all, which drew on Old Testament notions of sacrifice as a way of putting matters right between humanity and God. St Augustine defined sacrifice in this way: 'A true sacrifice is offered in every action which is designed to unite us to God in a Holy Fellowship.' But this was one of the highest points in a long and varied history. Many advocates of a sacrificial interpretation of the cross have hardly moved from the conceptual world of the books of Exodus and Leviticus, where the sacrificial system was first set out in detail. A development of the sacrificial scheme set out three elements of sacrifice – or rather of the priestly function within the sacrificial system. 'The prophetic office shows God to us; the priestly office leads us to God; and the office of king joins us together with God and glorifies us with him.'[10] In this system, Jesus is understood as prophet, priest and king. Sacrifice, in short, was the act of setting something aside as holy, or sacred; the way in which this was done was to offer it (an animal) to God by killing and burning it. In more recent history the sacrifice has come to be applied to the costly self-giving of Christ, rather than focusing on the death of a sacrificed animal.

But how does sacrifice – whether human or animal – help? To the modern mind this is a totally baffling idea. One possible way of getting our heads round it is to see that to offer a sacrifice in the form of the most valuable thing in one's possession (and in a pastoral culture the animals are the most valuable possessions by far) is to express how seriously we take the whole business of sin and putting it right. Taking life is itself a very serious business, for life is the gift of God – as indeed is the giving of life in the processes of conception and birth. Although we 'use' the lives of domestic ani-

10 François Turrettini, Genevan theologian, 1679.

mals for our human benefit, their life, which we have extinguished (or someone else has extinguished on our behalf) in order to feed ourselves – indeed all life – belongs in the realm of the transcendent rather than in the utilitarian world of our disposals. If all life belongs to God, then our life belongs to God. If we have lived as though that were not the case, it is hardly surprising that things have gone wrong, or that we feel ill-at-ease. This is why the early Church found the idea of sacrifice a fruitful source of ideas for interpreting the death of Jesus. Remember, however, that that is all they were trying to do – interpret the death of Jesus, answer the question 'Why did Jesus die?' It may be that we do not find their interpretation illuminating. Perhaps we find it repellent. But the problem remains: how *do* we interpret the death of Jesus?

A further group of theories is centred on the passage in Philippians 2 in which Paul writes of Jesus emptying himself (see vv. 6–11). Charles Wesley picks up this theme in his hymn 'And can it be . . .'.[11] In verse 3 he writes, of Jesus: '. . . emptied himself of all but love, and bled for Adam's helpless race'. Strictly speaking, this 'emptying' theory (often called the *kenotic* theory, from the Greek word *kenosis* = emptying) fills a larger canvas than just a theory of the atonement. It really amounts to a theory of (or way of looking at) the idea of incarnation, the idea that God could somehow become man, which is absolutely central to Christianity.

But it is not without its difficulties. The late D. Z. Phillips argued[12] that this kenotic theory leaves us with a real problem. If, in order to redeem humanity and present to us God's true loving nature, Jesus set aside his heavenly glory, and then, when that task was completed, returned to his former heavenly condition, which picture of God is the true one? Is it the 'self-sacrificing servant' picture of Jesus' earthly ministry, or is it his blissful heavenly condition to which he returned? Which one is 'the real deal'?

Another solution, which contrasts still more deeply with the sacrificial theories, was put forward by a bright young scholar of the eleventh and twelfth centuries, Peter Abelard. He argued

11 See *Hymns and Psalms*, Methodist Publishing House, 1983, no. 216.

12 D. Z. Phillips, *The Problem of Evil and the Problem of God*, London, SCM Press, 2004.

that the life and ministry of Christ was essentially one of moral example, and that the cross was the ultimate illustration of the love of God. Its effect was not to bring about some metaphysical change in the unseen universe, but to change human hearts and minds. This approach counters some of the concerns raised by the forensic theories (*forensic* = those based on the criminal court). However, many theologians, while accepting the value of this approach, remain hesitant about it because it seems to deny any objective effect to the cross. They want the cross to have changed something, to have some effect, independent of our response to it; 'It's not all in the mind', they want to argue. Here is the distinction between 'brought about' and 'offered'. Abelard's position is that Jesus *offered* to us what was already available had we but known it. His critics say that the death of Jesus also *brought about* something quite new.

One of the most controversial theories of atonement is that known as penal substitution. It's origins go back to St Paul, but its full development had to wait[13] until the second millennium. It is grounded in a view of sin as a grave offence to God's honour and therefore as demanding punishment – a punishment that human beings could not experience and survive. Under this view, the death of Jesus is one in which he received the punishment due to us. Penal substitution was only fully developed in its modern form, however, by an American theologian, Charles Hodge, writing in the nineteenth century. Many Christians regard it as the only trustworthy account of the matter, while others regard it with utter abhorrence – and, as might be expected, there are many positions in between those extremes. What is interesting, in view of the stridency with which its advocates sometimes proclaim this 'theory', is the fact that in terms of the history of Christian theology, it is something of a recent innovation!

There is a further notion to be drawn out of this question about the death of Jesus, which relates to the debates about the incarnation which raged in the early centuries of the Christian era. Remember the Gnostic/Docetic argument that because the

13 Many Christians will be rather startled to discover that this idea emerged so late; it is popularly understood to be the original authentic way of understanding the atonement.

material world is inherently evil there could be no question of God becoming man, let alone suffering human hostility and death? The violent death of Jesus was a necessary consequence of his total identification with the human condition. He couldn't opt out when the going became too tough.

The above is evidently nothing more than a summary of the most influential answers which have been suggested in response to the question: Why did Jesus die? For a modern survey of this subject see, for example, *Recovering the Scandal of the Cross.*[14] The two writers of this book present a most interesting perspective on the subject, drawing attention to the link between atonement and our Western view of crime and punishment, in which guilt and innocence are irreconcilable polar opposites. In a different culture such as that of Japan, the understanding of 'putting matters right' is quite different. Shame rather than guilt is the determining factor. The very diversity of these 'theories' surely warns us against accepting any one of them as the entire truth, to be upheld and defended against all other insights. It is possible to learn even from those with whom we disagree. Rarely are they completely in the wrong.

'he descended to the dead.'

Now we find the Creed going way beyond provable basic facts. Or do we? This clause was shifted into and out of the historical variants of the Creed until about 650 CE. And when it was 'in', several interpretations were possible, all based on those securely traditional ways of working with the Bible that we saw earlier in the section on biblical language, though some of them sit very uncomfortably with modern understanding.

The first, and simplest, interpretation is that it is no more than a further confirmation of Jesus' death. He descended to the place where all dead people are.

A second interpretation, however, is based on a biblical text (1 Peter 3.19), which declares that after his death (and before his

14 M. D. Baker and J. B. Green, *Recovering the Scandal of the Cross: The Atonement in New Testament and Contemporary Contexts*, Downers Grove, Illinois, InterVarsity Press, 2000.

resurrection) Jesus preached to the 'spirits in prison'. Who were these 'spirits in prison'? There are various interpretations, but one refers to a group of angelic beings ('sons of God') whose seduction of human women (Genesis 6.1–4) was seen as leading to the general moral downfall which, in turn, so the ancient story goes, led to the Flood. By preaching to them, Jesus affirmed his power to restore order to the spiritual realm.

In another interpretation, Jesus descended to preach to those people who had poured scorn on Noah's attempts to build a big boat to ensure his family's survival in the time of the Flood. This interpretation of Peter's words became attached to this clause in the Creed as a response (perhaps) to the question: What is the position of people who lived before Christ lived? How can they benefit from what Jesus did? In a highly symbolic way, this clause appears to be affirming that – in some way that is beyond our comprehension – even this conundrum can be solved. God's love as proclaimed in Jesus extends even to those who could never have known Jesus, and so could never have understood God to be like that – as Jesus portrayed him.

This transcendent-as-human, then, entered into the most profound depths of human experience. It was not a case of 'God in disguise', someone who could, like Sherlock Holmes, in a moment shed the moustaches, wig, shabby clothes and stooping gait of his subterfuge – to the astonishment of Dr Watson and Inspector Lestrade. Jesus was indeed fully human.

To put it another way: there is, therefore, no way of avoiding the reality of the transcendent, no human experience that can entirely hide it from view, because the whole range of human life and existence is suffused with it. 'The darkness could not overcome it.'[15]

Furthermore, the reach of the love of the transcendent is, literally, universal. It is not territorially bounded, limited to a domain that is familiar to us. Nor is it restricted to that segment of history which begins with the life of Jesus of Nazareth.

---

15 John 1.5 (NRSV).

Meaning

When the suffering is done, and all that is left is emptiness – what then? These are questions that beset millions caught up directly in catastrophes both natural and man-made, from floods to genocide. These questions also dog the footsteps of millions whose lives have escaped such trauma, but who wonder where these experiences can be fitted into a coherent understanding of the way things are. And as our own years accumulate, with some meagre scraps of gathered wisdom, some happy memories and some sad, we may wonder: What did that all add up to? What did it mean?

The stories surrounding the death of Jesus, and the events that some claimed to have witnessed in the following weeks, may be helpful to us as we struggle with these profound questions for ourselves.

'On the third day he rose again,'

A few days after his death, Jesus' closest associates reported seeing him alive. They were able to recount stories of appearances which were both familiar and strange. The person they 'saw' was sometimes recognizable as the Jesus they had known,[16] sometimes not. Sometimes he ate food, and otherwise behaved 'normally'; sometimes his appearances defied the constraints of time and place to which 'real people' are bound.

At its basic level, this claim is absurd. It presents us with a severe challenge. True, there are instances of people coming back to life again after being pronounced clinically dead (though not brain-dead), but such instances usually occur in the closely monitored confines of a hospital or an ambulance.

There are also records of people who report encounters with a recently dead loved one, often bearing messages of reassurance. In the Introduction to her book *The Origin of Satan*,[17] Elaine Pagels

16 See, for example, Luke 24.15–16, 36–42. John 20.11–18 describes one 'resurrection appearance' in which Jesus was not recognized immediately, perhaps because common sense ruled out the possibility of such an encounter. But later (20.19–21, 26; and 21.7) Jesus was recognized.

17 E. H. Pagels, *The Origin of Satan*, London, Allen Lane, 1996.

tells of her experience following the sudden death of her husband. 'I became aware that, like many people who grieve, I was living in the presence of an invisible being – living, that is, with a vivid sense of someone who had died.'

There are, however, no records of such presences eating food in company with the living. Furthermore, it would be very unusual for such appearances to be witnessed simultaneously by several people. People who have died and been buried for a couple of days do not get up and walk away.

Jesus did!

At least, that is what the simplest and most direct reading of the Gospels invites us to believe, and which this clause of the Creed invites us to believe. We have no means of establishing what happened that morning, just outside Jerusalem, apart from what the Gospels tell us. Option 2 (p. 24) of our original four – 'Take it all literally' – admits of no doubt: it happened, just like that.

But the accounts in the four Gospels are a bit patchy and do not always agree about details. Who was the first to see the risen Jesus? Was he instantly recognizable? Could he walk through closed doors? What does that say about his bodily nature? Could he eat food? Did he need to eat food? If so, how do we square that with the accounts of him walking through closed doors? Did the food he had eaten also pass through closed doors?

Some readers will immediately sense that I'm trying to argue that the Gospel accounts are unreliable and not to be believed. Not so! I'm simply pointing out that there are enough difficulties with a literal interpretation for us to be very cautious about the statement, 'It happened just like that.' Nor am I criticizing the Gospel writers for failing to ensure that their stories were consistent. If they were co-conspirators in a fraud, such a charge might perhaps stick, but they weren't. At the time they were overwhelmed by a transforming experience; decades later, when they wrote it all down, they were leading church communities scattered all over the Roman world – there was simply no possibility of such deliberately deceptive collusion.

So some of us ask instead: Is there a way of looking at this remarkable statement that makes complete sense without requiring us to believe the impossible?

There may be. From the perspective of *proof beyond reasonable doubt*, we may remain uneasy about a strictly literal interpretation, but we can agree that something very remarkable indeed must have taken place to transform a fairly ill-assorted bunch of people – easily capable, according to their track-record, of misunderstanding what Jesus was saying, and of acting in an utterly cowardly manner – into the effective founders of the Church against all opposition.

That 'something' may have been exactly as the Gospels appear to describe it – we cannot *know* – but could also have been a collective experience of 'penny dropping' on an unparalleled scale, in which the penny dropped almost simultaneously, and dramatically, for a whole group of people. The 'dropping penny', of course, is the profound insight into the nature of Jesus that we tried to unpack in an earlier section ('I believe in Jesus Christ'). He was not a human martyr, not a failed revolutionary, not someone who was too nice for his own good (to mention just a few of many similar hypotheses). None of those tags matches the disciples' total experience of this man, both before and after his death.

We cannot leave this clause without some consideration of 'the third day'. Jews believed that it was on the third day after death that the soul finally left the body and that physical life was irrecoverably extinct. Here again, then, is a further underscore to the assertion that Jesus really, truly died.

Is Jesus still with us?

We raised this question in a footnote to the section headed 'he was conceived by the Holy Spirit'. Like the claim that Jesus rose from the dead, this seems patently absurd. Examine the DNA of every living person and you will not find Jesus. He is not here. The phrase 'ascended into heaven' (which comes a little later) will provide a further reminder that we are on the wrong track if we think of the presence of Jesus in that sort of way – looking for an individual who is identifiably 'Jesus'. Such an identification would necessarily entail this individual – and therefore the presence of Jesus – being confined to one place at any given moment.

As we noted earlier, it is very important to Christians that – in some sense – Jesus is still with us. I take this to mean that the experience which transformed the lives of a terrified and traumatized group of Jesus' friends, in the weeks between Easter and Pentecost, is one that is experienced by Christians today, despite the fact that today's believers do not have the background of having known Jesus as an individual human being. Nor do modern Christians share with those first-century Christians the cultural background of Jewishness which was influential in determining the form their faith took.

Three things need to be said about this claim.

First, when it is transmuted into a simple 'Jesus is alive' it is plainly metaphorical. The word 'alive' is strongly suggestive of warm flesh and blood, breathing, tangible, electrical activity in the brain, 'vital signs' and so on. (To avoid the grave charge of speciesism I must assure the reader that these vital signs apply to any other warm-blooded organism; other tests, no doubt, would apply to fish, reptiles, plants and so on.) These are attributes of a physical body. But which physical body are we talking about when we assert that 'Jesus is alive'? There is no such body. So, when we refer to Jesus as 'alive' we must mean something other than 'There is a physical body of a person named Jesus which is alive, breathing, having an active brain, etc.'

So, what *do* we mean? We might mean something like, 'His spirit lives on in the community of people who follow him.' Indeed, this is arguably the Christian position on this question, following Paul's assertion, 'You are the body of Christ.' Jesus is alive in the sense that his Spirit lives in those who believe in him (i.e. those who trust him and are committed to him). They, his followers, are the most authentic evidence that 'he lives'. But is this different from, say, 'The spirit of Mozart lives on in the lives of musicians who interpret his music'? While not denying that claim about the spirit of Mozart, Christians would hold that there is a huge difference between those two claims.

Second, it doesn't really simplify matters at all. It nudges the problem sideways a bit, but it doesn't explain anything. Think about it: here we have two sets of experiences: one (call it A) shared by the friends of Jesus in New Testament times; and one (call it B) known to Christian believers today. The claim is that these are the same experiences – or at least, experiences of essentially the same kind. The logical problem here arises because it is not clear whether we are arguing from A to B or from B to A; is experience B comparable to A (and therefore an experience of the transcendent as known in Jesus of Nazareth); or is it that experience A is comparable to experience B (and therefore something we ourselves can relate to)?

Third, it is *only in principle* a universally accessible experience. If through my living-room window I see a spectacular sunset, I can call my wife to join me confident that she will also see a spectacular sunset. She can 'manufacture' for herself an experience akin to mine simply by coming to the appropriate window and looking out. Experience B is not like that. It cannot be manufactured; indeed, if it were capable of being manufactured, it would probably be suspect. This is, of course, one reason why the language of science and the language of religious belief do not sit comfortably together in the same sentence; the whole point of a scientific experience, i.e. an experiment with a certain outcome, is that it *can* be manufactured. What can be manufactured, however, is only *the outcome of the experiment*, the observations that confirm a previously published result. What *cannot* be manufactured is the awesome thrill felt by the originator of this scientific insight when his experiment first worked. Even the most ardently atheist scientists wax lyrical in their reports of this phenomenon. A central Christian claim, however, is that theirs really is *potentially* a universal experience – as John Wesley wrote, 'All men can know that they are saved.' (Pardon the religious language.)

Truth to tell, the tags A and B we have used to denote experiences of 'the risen Jesus whom we knew before' and 'the Jesus who we believe is still with us' are much more complex than this very simple analysis might suggest. These experiences are (and were) extremely varied. We might call them B, B', B'', B''' and so on. One of the problems with religion is that individuals and groups whose version of experience B is sufficiently coherent have a marked inclination to disparage and devalue anyone else's version of experience B. Experience B can well be termed 'irregular'; it cannot readily be brought into a manageable framework, in interesting contrast to the biblical claims about the orderliness of the universe (and where would science be without that belief in orderliness?).

There is a further corollary of this 'irregularity' of experience B. It is that we know this experience as a 'given' – not in the sense of a mathematical axiom that does not need to be proved logically, but in the sense that its coming is something over which we have no control; it is a gift. For more on this, see below, in Chapter 8, under 'Grace'.

Recall for a moment my earlier remark about the Spirit of Jesus and the spirit of Mozart. I claimed that (at least so Christians believe) there is a huge difference between them. We cannot simply slip away into the darkness and pretend that this point has not been raised.

Interpreters of Mozart's music come from a very select group of people. Their level of technical proficiency is outstandingly high, in the sense that their hands or voices can produce the sounds their brains direct them to. Through a lifetime of study, they also have a deep understanding of what Mozart may have been trying to say.

Some of the people who listen to Mozart's music are inspired thereby to pursue worthy objectives and are supported in their endeavours by their acquaintance with that music, even if they are unable to interpret the music for themselves. For them, the music of Mozart is akin to a sacred place; exposure to his music reveals the transcendent.

The interpreters of Mozart's music are musicians. They can and do interpret the music of other composers. Alongside Mozart they reverence and perform the works of Bach, Handel, Beethoven, Schubert, Brahms, Mahler and many others. Their personal response to these composers may be rather different, giving them a special affinity for one composer over the others, and hence a reputation for particularly fine interpretations of that composer's music.

It is this last characteristic that forms the basis (I suspect) for the distinction that many Christians are trying to draw. There is an exclusive character about religious commitments, at least under the Christian, Jewish and Muslim banners. If, as Jesus remarked, you cannot serve God and Mammon, then neither can you serve more than one God; this is in fact a central tenet of all three Abrahamic faiths. Sadly, the prohibition against worshipping other gods has led to much bigotry, as believers of all persuasions fail to recognize the character of the one God in the adherents of a faith other than their own.

We need to say one more thing about this idea that Jesus is alive in Spirit in his followers. We must in all honesty acknowledge that although the followers of Jesus may include some who in a truly astonishing way reflect the Spirit of Jesus, there are also many who do not. This sad fact certainly leaves no room for Christian pride or complacency, nor for arrogant assumptions about the moral worth of people who profess no faith; but it also holds another meaning for Christians. People who go to court to settle disputes are increasingly doing so without the benefit of professional legal counsel. Most people who have tried to do this later agree with those who say they would have been wiser to entrust their cause to a professional team. God has, in effect, entrusted the advocacy of his cause to a very mixed bunch of people, some utterly awe-inspiring in their lives, others very mediocre indeed, some very dubious. It is almost as if getting us to raise our game is more important to God than having the best available defence team to defend God's reputation.

Why is the resurrection so important?

The first sermons (or speeches) given by the leading figures among Jesus' followers had one central message: 'This Jesus, whom you crucified, God has raised from death, for death could not hold him.' At a number of points in his letters to his churches, Paul lays great stress on the resurrection, emphasizing that it did actually happen, that people witnessed the events that followed (we call them 'the post-resurrection appearances'), and that the faith of the Christians to whom he was writing – and indeed his own faith – rested squarely on the historical truth of what he described.

In effect, Paul was describing a chain of belief that began with evidence of the resurrection and leads through the credibility of the first witnesses, through the work and activity of the Christian communities that made up the Church, and ends with the faith-commitment of ordinary Christians. In doing so, he created a logical structure that depended crucially upon its opening premiss – that the resurrection of Jesus did actually happen as described by those who were there and saw it.

Clearly such a chain of logic falls apart if that initial premiss is not in fact true as he stated; it becomes a rope of sand. Paul admitted as much himself: 'If Christ is not raised . . . we are of all people most to be pitied' (1 Cor. 17–19, NRSV).

It is possible, however, to look at this chain of logic in a different way. After all, Paul's central claim rests upon the reliability, the trustworthiness of those first witnesses. If they were not reliable or trustworthy, then their testimony can be dismissed as unsatisfactory and their claims rejected. In the middle of his argument, Paul makes a very strong and surprising personal claim: that the testimony of those first witnesses was corroborated (for Paul) by the direct endorsement of God himself, thus placing Paul himself, in effect, among those first witnesses.

Here, Paul is attempting to sidestep the criticism that 'we only have your word for it'. His readers in Corinth were being invited, it seemed, to believe that the resurrection actually happened because the first witnesses were the revered leaders of the Christian movement. Paul, in their eyes, wasn't one of those first witnesses; how, then, can they believe him? He may have been giving a false account of what those first witnesses had reported. Paul's claim, however, is that because he learned of the resurrection by revelation from God, his testimony is as good as that of those primary witnesses. The people in the communities Paul had founded and which remained in his pastoral care have been willing to invest sufficient trust in his words to persuade them to become Christians. They were sufficiently confident of his integrity to commit themselves to the Christian way as a result of hearing his arguments and testimony. They should, therefore, accept his claim to be in effect a primary witness alongside Peter and John and Mary and the others. It was, for Paul, an issue of confidence in his apostolic authority.

So, the focus has shifted from the (alleged) original events, first to the primary witnesses whose accounts convinced many to believe that those original events did indeed take place and so to become Christians, and then to Paul who, though not strictly a primary witness, claimed that status as a 'special case'. The readers of Paul's letters (or rather, the hearers; few would have been able to read or even to have ready access to a physical copy of the letters) were thus invited to believe not because of the original events, but because of the testimony of reliable witnesses, or else because of the testimony of Paul whose words they had already found convincing. This seems to make the key assertion – that the resurrection did indeed happen – dependent on the trustworthiness of a succession of witnesses who can speak of their personal experiences (our 'experience B'), all of which point to the fact of Jesus' resurrection (or at least to the reliability of those original first-hand accounts of 'experience A'). This chain of logic can be extended through many generations to us – to you and to me.

Why do we believe the stories of the resurrection? Because they were described in written accounts by trustworthy witnesses.

Why do we regard them as trustworthy witnesses? Because their followers, who have taught us the faith and whose integrity in these matters we accept, assure us that they were trustworthy witnesses.

Why do we hold that the people who have taught and nurtured our faith are themselves people of integrity and therefore to be trusted? Because through them we have come to an experience of our own which is in accord with what they have told us.

We may now pull at this chain of logic from the other end, so to speak, and make a claim that is slightly different from the one Paul was encouraging his correspondents to accept. To them he said, in effect: 'Believe me; you can rely upon the word of those first witnesses; Jesus was raised from the dead.' Instead we may argue that what is most important for us is our own personal experience. Because our experience matches what others have told us, it encourages us to place our trust in their testimony. And at least in principle this extension of trust goes back to the first witnesses whose account of the empty tomb and the resurrection appearances formed the basis of early Christianity.

Destiny

In our musings on those ultimate questions about the meaning of life, are we simply arriving at a state of mind that represents a degree of inner contentment at the answer, a private assessment of our condition? Or is there any possibility that there might be a detached, objective standpoint from which someone can take stock of the bag of jumble with which we arrive at the end of our days? And which someone? Can we trust their judgement, or is their perspective as subject as ours is to distortion and bias? If our spectacles are rose-tinted, how do we know that the other person's spectacles aren't tinted blue, or green? If we have begun to relate to the story of Jesus in a particular way – I have ventured to call it a mythic way (while hedging that word about with careful defences against its too-easy misuse) – what is the ultimate test, the ultimate validation of that relationship?

'he ascended into heaven,'

Here we take the theme of Jesus' ultimate significance, to which brief reference was made earlier, under the heading 'Is Jesus still with us?'. In the Jewish cosmology, heaven was 'up', so getting to heaven required one to ascend. But what exactly is the significance of heaven, here? This too we have touched on earlier, in the section headed 'creator of heaven and earth'.

This is the ultimate vindication of everything that Jesus stood for and tried to accomplish – that he should ascend to heaven, there to share in his father's approval, resuming his place at the father's right hand. This is, of course, metaphorical language, a fact which Yuri Gagarin conspicuously failed to appreciate when he is alleged to have reported, on his return to earth after his single orbit of the planet, that he hadn't found God 'up there'. (It has been suggested that these words were not in fact those of Gagarin himself, but of Nikita Krushchev, the Soviet Premier.)

As we saw earlier, D. Z. Phillips[18] has argued that there is a problem with this description of the life of Jesus – pre-existent

18 Phillips, *Problem of Evil.*

in heaven, becoming truly human for our salvation, ascending to heaven to resume his former glory. It is this: a story in which, in the end, Jesus simply goes back to the *status quo ante* invites the question: Is the incarnation real, or is it a con trick? Which is the real deal, Jesus in heaven or Jesus caught up in the toils of human struggle? By emphasizing Jesus' ascension, the Creed solves one problem (yes, the work is done and vindicated by God himself), but at the cost of raising another (blink and you've missed him; was he really here; is he really one of us?).

There may be very good reasons for taking Phillips' concerns seriously, but they lie elsewhere. Perhaps we don't need to go as far as Phillips wants to take us – at least, not in the present context. I remember once reading a book of good advice to young ministers. It included a remarkably simple tip for ending a pastoral visit. Say goodbye, get up and go. It's a signal that the purposes of your visit have been achieved and it is time to bring it to an end. A decisive departure may be taken as a signal that the job is done. Perhaps that is another part of the significance of 'vindication' in our reading of this clause of the Creed. Whatever the intended content of Jesus' life and ministry might have been, the Ascension is a clear sign that it has been done. There is nothing more to add.

This, however, doesn't silence the questioning mind. What is it that has now been completed? What is it to which nothing can now be added? In traditional Christian interpretations of the life of Jesus, this has to do with the meaning of the crucifixion. We have begun to discuss this in the section 'suffered under Pontius Pilate'.

Recall if you will another discussion, where we were dealing with the birth of Jesus. We suggested that these wonderful stories might be a metaphorical way of reminding us that the transcendent, however vast the canvas on which we might project it, belongs also in the human dimension.[19] A single human life *can* realize transcendence, *can* embody the transcendent. This is such a remarkable claim that it needs to be rendered specifically in a particular human life. Broad general principles, however strongly supported by theory, need to be substantiated in at least one par-

19 It might be even better to suggest that the transcendent dimension *intersects* the human dimension.

ticular instance. Only in this way can they leave behind the realm of speculation and become real. The Christian claim is that in the life of Jesus we see that particular human life. His vindication, therefore, as signalled in the resurrection and the Ascension, amounts to a confirmation that nothing more needs to be done to complete this demonstration, that a human life *can* transcend the limitations of humanness.

We may then ask: Where is all this leading? What is the point? What might it mean for human lives to transcend themselves? In our earlier discussion of transcendence we were clearly attaching a moral value to transcendence. Extreme cruelty might well take an individual far beyond the bounds of normal human behaviour, but we would surely be reluctant to use the word 'transcendent' to describe it. To excel in cruelty seems a contradiction in terms. For most people, cruelty is not 'excellent' in any way.

The Christian claim is that the life and death of Jesus together express this notion of excellence or transcendence in two senses. First: the life and death of Jesus declare the possibility of transcendence. And second, they show us the direction in which we ourselves should search for excellence.

Yes, we should pursue excellence. The vindication inherent in the Ascension of Jesus is surely a signal that the enterprise of excellence is now our human responsibility. Jesus has underlined the possibility and pointed out our goal. Now the task is ours. But the Christian tradition reminds us that God has provided not only the commission and the direction, but also the resources.

'he is seated at the right hand of the Father,'

Picture if you will a Bedouin tent. It is square and has vertical walls, more like a modern frame tent than a ridge tent. In the middle are tables of food and jugs of cardamom coffee. Around the walls are low, cushioned seats. In the place of honour sits the father of the tribe. On his left is the guest of honour; on his right is his eldest son. This displays the fact that the patriarch has an heir; his realm is secure; there is no question of disputed succession. Let no one challenge the decision of the head of the family. It also tells the assembled company that *this* man is his heir, his chosen successor; *this* man carries the patriarch's authority. In giving him the unique place at his right hand, the father is honouring his son, celebrating the work his son has done in creating and sustaining the wealth and reputation of the family, and signalling his trust in the son to continue the good work. He is indeed a worthy successor.

This feast, though, is also a time of rest from work, a time of hospitality, welcome and celebration, of gathering and fellowship, of trust and mutual confidence.

Something of this picture is evoked by these words of our Creed. It is a public announcement, by the father, of the high regard in which the son is held. In Christian thinking it is a way of proclaiming the divine nature of Jesus. No doubt it reeks of patriarchy in ways that many find offensive (as we have said earlier), but let us hear the meaning it conveyed to the first users of this language rather than the offence given to our more refined sensibilities!

John's Gospel is full of statements and sayings that carry this same message.[20] At heart, John is boldly asserting this claim: in Jesus we see God. What is more, we see in Jesus as much as we can grasp, or understand, or cope with, of a *complete vision of God*. Moreover, when we look at Jesus we get no misleading impressions. In Jesus we see the truth, the whole truth (well, as much as we can make any kind of sense of) and nothing but the truth – about God.

John 5 sets out the relationship between Jesus and God. We are told that the son does nothing but what he sees the father doing. If you think about it, this is a very domestic image of a child imitating a parent's behaviour. It also echoes what might have happened in the carpenter's shop in Nazareth, as Joseph taught the young Jesus his trade. So, here is one of many affirmations by the Gospel writer of the unique, exalted status of Jesus.

Our Creed proclaims this loud and clear, though in different language. In saying this part of the Creed, we are honouring and affirming our belief in Jesus as the one who has brought home to us the truth of God, so perfectly that in our consciousness we

20 See, for example, John 14.8.

cannot separate him from God. But in the terms of our Creed, it isn't set in the future at the end of time. Its hour is *now*. The moment of truth!

'and he will come to judge the living and the dead.'

But this picture is a static one, like one of those posed Victorian family portraits, with the father upright in his best suit, bearded and moustachioed, mother in black bombazine, children in sailor suits and dresses of laced cotton, all stiff and humourless, struggling to keep quite still for the long exposures required. The Creed goes on to remind us that this is not an ancient portrait in the divine family album at all. The characters are very much alive, and will certainly spring out of the frame to surprise us.

Earlier we pointed out that the shape of the Creed is that of a story. In this it resembles the main ingredient of popular entertainment – for example, on television. I remember my father expressing dismay at the way some stories end. He complained that they didn't seem to have an ending. By this, I suspect he might have meant that questions were unresolved, or that loose ends were left lying around. The storyteller does indeed have a delicate balancing act to perform here. On the one hand the story has to offer closure by settling the immediate questions: Who committed the crime? Will he recover from his illness? Will the business succeed?

On the other hand, the good storyteller may also want to convey the sense of an ongoing story. She may wish to impress upon her readers the idea that her characters were not created out of nothing for the purposes of this story, nor are they to be dropped into the wastebasket when the action is over. Her characters gain credibility from the idea, however slight the hints may be, that they have a life outside this story; this story is only one strand of a bigger story, the rest of which is real but doesn't concern us here. They come with a background, and their lives will go on. Indeed, if the form of the story is that of a television series which the viewers have enjoyed and with whose leading characters they have identified, they will look for clues that might help them answer the question: 'Is there going to be another series next year?'

There is also a further complication in modern storytelling (which may, for all I know, stand in an ancient tradition of live storytelling). It is the idea that readers or viewers can exercise some control about the turning-points in the story, inviting the players or the characters to offer alternative narratives. How would things turn out if the heroine were to walk past the restaurant instead of going into it?

The claim of the Creed, however, is that it *is* the big picture; it is life, not a part of life. There is no 'life outside this story'. On the contrary, this is the context from which we are all invited to draw meaning for our ongoing lives. And a key part of the way the story ends relates to how we make our choices as the story unfolds.

How do we address questions like these, in relation to the Creed? Not least among the problems involved in responding to this question is the fact that we, the observers, are ourselves in the middle of the story. In hinting at the ending, the Creed story is taking us way outside our experience into a realm for which we have no map, no guidebook, no phrasebook. The best it can do is to give us clues. So, what are those clues?

Don't ask me how or why that is; it's one of the many loose ends that everyone who affirms the Creed will spend a lifetime pondering. The Ascension is not the end of the story but the beginning of a new chapter, a chapter in which we now understand God in Jesus to be closely involved in our lives.

John 3.17 states: 'For God sent not his Son into the world to condemn the world; but that the world through him might be saved (AV).' Some translations say 'condemn', others say 'judge'. The Greek word is *κρινω*, which can mean condemn, but more usually means 'investigate with a view to reaching a verdict'. 'He will come . . .' simply assures us that in some way Jesus is central to the way the story will unfold. He remains intensely interested in us, in our future, in the course of our life, in the pattern of our being. And his objective is in some sense to keep God's project on track – not by eliminating or even constraining our choices, but by coping with the consequences of our bad calls as well as delighting in our better ones. As part of that 'coping', together with God's commitment to our flourishing, we need to understand that our choices matter.

God's Son was sent into the world not to judge, not to condemn, but to bring good news to God's people, to bring salvation, to enable us to take up his own pursuit of excellence.

So, the purpose of Jesus' earthly ministry was not condemnation or judgement at all. The business of judgement in that sense (surprisingly, when you think it through) is in our own hands. The mission of Jesus was to set before us the critical decision, to put in place the means by which we can see clearly the right decision to make. Humanity has a talent for inviting catastrophe by making the decision that is most harmful to it. Jesus' purpose was to save, to rescue humanity from that talent for self-destruction while in no way diluting our freedom or our responsibility in the choices we make.

But here, in the Creed, we're talking about Jesus judging the living and the dead. We are, here, talking about the last word (remember what we said about 'the last word', in Chapter 1 on metaphor?). For this phrase in the Creed is telling us something about God's values, about what is important to God. And what is that? It is God's great project: living creatures with spirit, able to return God's love, able to enjoy fellowship with God, able to share in God's purpose, able to choose. In God's terms, our freedom to choose is absolutely crucial. The choices are vast, and we get confused, and we often make the wrong decisions. But God can cope.

So, what's going on in this judging of the living and the dead? Some years ago there were worrying inconsistencies in the judging at the Winter Olympic Games. There'll be no inconsistency at the last judgement! This judgement to come is a revealing of God's values, a disclosure of the clues that will enable us to know how to decide. In all our life's decision-making there are deeply puzzling shades of grey. This moment of judgement is when our perplexity about these shades of grey is resolved, clearly, once and for all.

The dead – those who have long been dead – are involved too. They too will receive this judgement. There's no avoiding it. Truth has to be faced at some point. Some choose to see that point as the moment when God condemns the wicked. Others see it as the moment when at last all the suspense is over, the truth is revealed, and the questions are answered. But whatever our view of this, we should never forget those words of Jesus; that the condemnation comes in essence from our own response to the love of God.

Implied in this idea of a 'last judgement' there is something a bit tricky that we have to find our way through. Educators talk of two kinds of assessment: 'formative assessment', which is when homework is marked so that the student is advised about strengths and weaknesses and encouraged to do even better; and 'summative assessment', which is the final outcome of the module or the course, telling everyone whether they have passed or not.

But each of these forms of assessment implies a future. Formative assessment implies that you continue on the course so that the corrective measures can have their effect and your performance can improve. Summative assessment opens the door to using your hard-won qualification in practising as a plumber, electrician, teacher, doctor, engineer (or minister of religion!). So, is this 'last judgement' formative or summative? The label 'last' suggests that this assessment cannot possibly be formative, because (we suppose) there is no future at all. For God to reveal the crib sheet after the exam seems heartless and cruel.

Perhaps we're thinking along the wrong track altogether in supposing that there is no future. The Christian tradition (among others) claims the contrary, that there is a future, and the key point at issue is whether, in the course of life on earth, we have learned anything about how to relate to the transcendent (God). The future, according to this tradition, is one in which the fruits of that learning are harvested. It is a happy future if we have learned well; unhappy if we have not. But in our lives we are far from equal. Here is a child in her early teens, abused by her father for several years. He is now in prison for the offence, but no one has helped her put her life and her self back together again. Her opportunities for learning how to relate to God are very narrow indeed, compared with her more fortunate contemporaries. Their learning environments are separated by an almost unbridgeable gulf.

But still we're not through. Of that future we know nothing except as a matter of faith, of trust. We have not even a smidgen of a hint about such questions as these. How is this 'last judgement' to take account of the gulf between one person's learning opportunities and another's? Will this future – for all of us – include further opportunity for learning and growth? We might wish to argue that a life without such opportunities would be paltry and pinched. We might wish to argue that a God of love couldn't possibly have in store for us such a miserable destiny. But we do not have any settled information, no certainty except that of trust – which is all we have when we embark on the great adventure of life itself. The Christian tradition proclaims the clue to the nature of that trust: in Jesus we see God's love revealed.

It is that trust in Jesus, and through him in God, that constitutes the ground for our hope that there is an answer to imponderable questions like that of the abused girl left to fend, emotionally, for herself. But that trust motivates and enables the people of Jesus to want to do something about her situation. It is not enough to deplore what has happened. If the Christian claim about a God of love means anything at all, it must surely mean taking steps to bring about change.

7

The Holy Spirit

We have followed the story of Jesus, as rehearsed in the Apostles' Creed. To our explorations we have brought our questions – many of them, deep and varied. Some of them have perhaps been answered, but some have not, and in all probability new questions will have taken hold in our minds. That is the nature of the ongoing journey of life: wrestling with questions.

Perhaps at this point, however, it would be good to pause and take stock. Yet again a chorus of questioning voices can be heard. Isn't all this just a matter of what's happening between my ears? I can respond to it as a story, or a myth (again, remember what we mean by myth). Responding to it may indeed prove helpful to me when I am 'down'. But is this all there is to it? Is there anywhere I can look for confirmation? How have other people responded to this story? Can I calibrate my response in relation to theirs?

There is, then, a sense in which this story is made available to us in such a way that we can appropriate it for ourselves, in relation both to God and to those other people who are trying, in their different ways, to do the same. The Creed expresses this in the clauses about the Holy Spirit. But this part of the Creed goes rather further.

Who?

'I believe in the Holy Spirit,'

About seven weeks or so after the resurrection, the friends of Jesus experienced a remarkable and dramatic personal transformation, as a result of which *dozens* of preachers and miracle-workers were in circulation, and not just *one* of them! Despite violent persecution, their message spread rapidly during the succeeding decades. This transforming experience is known to Christians as the giving of the Holy Spirit at Pentecost.

Short, they say, is sweet. Well, the people who compiled the Apostles' Creed were certainly sweet on the Holy Spirit. The Spirit gets just one line, and no detail at all.

In terms of the formation of the Creed, we have already referred to the theological controversies about whether or not the material world is inherently evil, and the implications of that for our understanding of Jesus. It is hardly surprising that a similar level of dispute surrounded the Holy Spirit. In the Nicene Creed this controversy too is nailed into its coffin. For now, however, the Holy Spirit is simply asserted as being on a par with God and Jesus. There is, of course, that 'and' (see above at the beginning of Chapter 6 on Jesus): 'I believe in God . . . *and* in Jesus Christ his Son.' The Holy Spirit is not granted this ambiguous elevation to equality with the Father, but is certainly grouped in the inner circle.

The people of Haiti believe in an all-powerful God who rules by decree and cares nothing for the personal circumstances of ordinary people. There is no point in worshipping such a God, as he is utterly remote and has no interest in them, so instead the people seek the help and guidance of a variety of spirits. This form of religion is known as animism.

This pattern – or something like it – is repeated in many cultures. A Creator God of supreme power is the ultimate ruler of the universe, the ultimate master of its destiny. But for the practical purposes of day-to-day life, a more user-friendly God is required, one to whom ordinary people can relate.

Perhaps rather surprisingly, this was also true of the cultures that surrounded the Children of Israel. The distinctive religious insight of the Jews was to realize (after centuries of struggling with the ideas) that there is only one God. The *Creator* God is also the *Covenant* God, who guides and guards, protects and corrects his people, taking a close interest in their individual and community life.

Even in the time of Jesus, however, this was a live issue. How can the God of absolutely everything have a meaningful relationship with one people, let alone one person? The solution that evolved in Christianity was the teaching we know as the doctrine of the Trinity. God is the creator of everything and the Father of all people; furthermore, in Jesus we see God in human shape living a life in which the relationship with the Father was plain for all to see, while in the Holy Spirit, God is working creatively and positively in our personal and community life.

One God.

So, no need for a multiplicity of user-friendly spirits attached to every place and every human activity, every season and every mood.

What, then, of this Holy Spirit? Can we unpack this part of the Creed while following the pattern of metaphor?

The doctrine of the Holy Spirit is one way of grappling with a profound idea, that in some way the transcendent addresses us, influences us, enables us. In conversation once with an atheist academic colleague, I had the greatest difficulty in convincing her that there is anything at all to this faith business. At one point, however, I suggested that a central idea is that of being addressed, being spoken to. Her reaction suggested acknowledgement that there might be something in it after all.

Of course it is easy to dismiss such a notion as bordering on dangerous lunacy. No doubt some readers will do so with glee. People who hear voices in their heads are understandably viewed with deep suspicion; many have done dreadful things to others. Underlying the doctrine of the Holy Spirit, however, is a conviction that all our human faculties of creativity and empathy, our sense of awe and wonder at the marvels of the natural world, our groping towards human fulfilment, and our struggles with faith – all these are the result of our being addressed, and beckoned, by the transcendent. For Christians, it is through the Holy Spirit that these impulses and drives come. Let's take a look at the biblical grounding of these ideas.

First, *the Holy Spirit is creative*. In Genesis the Spirit, *ruach*, moves over the face of the waters, bringing order out of chaos. Here the Spirit appears to be acting as God's agent, bringing about

God's design for the creation. But of course that is misleading, for the Spirit is not some lesser being other than God; the Spirit is God. In the Nicene Creed, the rather fuller statement describes the Holy Spirit as 'The Lord, the Giver of Life'.

Second, *the Holy Spirit is formative.* The Spirit points to Jesus as giving us the most accessible picture of God's healing and redeeming power. The Spirit points to the life of Jesus as the way to follow, and to Jesus as the one in whom to place our trust for life itself.

Third, *the Holy Spirit illuminates and guides.* In our journey through life there are opportunities and challenges, and there are threats to our well-being. The Holy Spirit discloses to us the truth about our situation and enables us to see a way forward. The Holy Spirit creates openings for us to show God's care for people. The Holy Spirit cuts through the fogs of fashion and the mire of controversy and enables us to see with clarity the issues that really count.

Fourth, *the Holy Spirit empowers.* God's great love is wholeness of individuals and communities. God's delight is our free and loving response to God's creating power and God's watchful love. And God gives us the gifts we need to exercise in order for that to happen, for the building up both of our individual selves and of the community.

Fifth, *the Holy Spirit is the communicator* who speaks to us of the love of God, and who enables us to say to God what we need to say when words fail us. What should we pray for when someone has set his heart on a decision that we can see will bring only disaster, and has asked us to pray for success? What should we pray for when a carer is struggling with the constriction of life imposed by the demands of a helpless invalid, longing for a peaceful end yet fearful of the guilt that such longings carry with them. Just as we spoke of a mysterious yet benign sense in which God addresses us, so we speak – no less mysteriously – of God enabling us to speak to him.

The Christian understanding of God as Father, Son and Holy Spirit is at one with Judaism and Islam in insisting that the awesome creator (creative? creating?) God, and the God of healing and mercy, are one and the same. One God. Yet this central

Christian teaching gives us the gift of intimacy with a God who understands our humanity because in Jesus God has *been* there; we *know* that God has been there; and God nurtures our growing relationship with Godself, tending the flame within us.

The late Canon David Watson once described the gift of the Holy Spirit as God's Kiss – a colourful, perhaps startling image, yet one that captures this sense of an intimacy with God that is at one and the same time uniquely and pricelessly our very own, yet also a relationship in which we know others can participate in their own distinctive way. So you and I each can know we are truly loved by God, yet we know also that God loves others with equal tenderness, understanding and intimacy.

I believe in the Holy Spirit.

The Church now

'(I believe in) the holy catholic Church,'

In the previous section, I remarked that the Holy Spirit gets just one line in the Creed. That isn't strictly true, of course. All the clauses described in this chapter are essentially the work of the Holy Spirit on the human plane.

In an earlier chapter we have suggested that religious experience is about the sense of being addressed as persons. We have also seen that our sensitivity to the transcendent – our degree of openness to the experiences of transcendence that may come our way – is linked to the kind of people we are, the way we treat other people, and even the way we treat ourselves. When a man asked Jesus, 'What must I do to be saved?' Jesus' answer was that 'You should love the Lord your God with all your heart, mind, soul and strength, and your neighbour as yourself.' In fact this was an impeccable response, according to the Jewish tradition. Full marks to Jesus for a perfect answer! And full marks to Jesus (and to his tradition) for saying it so very clearly; this is the link I'm talking about!

At this point I hear the indignant cries of atheists raised in vehement protest against what my words might be taken to imply.

The central question here is this: Is there really a link between morality and belief? Is it true to claim that *only* those who 'love the Lord their God with all their heart etc.' treat other people and themselves in a morally worthy way?

Some religious people might make this claim, but I do not, and I don't think that any creed makes this claim either. As we saw right at the beginning of this journey through the Creed, we must concede, however painful the admission might be, that religious people often – far too often – get it all hideously wrong. Some religious people are undoubtedly guilty of appalling behaviour towards others, both positive and negative. By 'appalling positive behaviour' I mean that some religious people find within their faith-tradition reasons to oppress and persecute others who do not agree with them. By 'appalling negative behaviour' I mean that religious arguments have sometimes been used to justify the denial of plain justice to people who are being oppressed by others.

Since the emergence of Methodism in the mid-eighteenth century, Methodists have regarded the relationship with God in very personal terms. Every year, usually in early January, they are invited to renew their covenant with God. The words of this service, in a text sadly no longer used, invited us to confess how 'we have borne so lightly wrongs and sufferings that were not our own'. How exactly those words capture that deplorable readiness to deny plain justice to the oppressed!

No, religious believers are not paragons. Nor do they have a monopoly of virtue. In our debates and discussions with people whose basic position is that religion is both nonsensical and harmful, we must accept the force of their evidence-based arguments if we expect the debate to be fruitful for anyone. (Sadly, the recent publications of the New Atheists during 2006 and 2007 mingle entirely legitimate criticisms of religious communities with outbursts of what appears to be blind prejudice.) Nor, I submit, should we wriggle and squirm by claiming that religious belief somehow adds to our moral life a quality not possessed or exhibited by unbelievers. There are, among believers and unbelievers alike, folk honestly struggling with the problems of how to live well, as well as folk to whom these questions are of no importance whatsoever, either in theory or in practice.

So what can we say about religion and the moral life? I think we can cautiously advance a claim that links our sensitivity to the transcendent (whether we experience this in the appreciation of music or in the 'Eureka!' moments of scientific discovery – or in the thousands of other categories of human endeavour, including religion) with the way we treat other people and even ourselves. This is far from being conclusive proof of anything; but it seems to be a fruitful avenue to pursue.

'The kingdom of God' is a phrase used to denote a time (or a condition of humanity) in which this link is complete and strong, in which people are in tune with the awesome transcendent (whatever picture of that we might build in our minds) and in tune with one another, responding to one another's laughter and tears as God would wish.

The Church is not the kingdom of God; the Church has never made such a claim. It is not a company of perfect people, model citizens of God's kingdom, flawless in every detail of belief and behaviour. It is, however, a company of people who have themselves been touched and transformed (more precisely, who *are being transformed*) by the values and 'style' of the kingdom of God. They are focused on a goal, looking every day for signs of that hidden reality in the lives of their fellow human beings (whether believers or not), and they can confidently point to those examples in encouragement and celebration. In their life together in local churches and in denominations, Christians try to build and operate structures that reflect the values of God's kingdom. In the ways in which they interact with their contemporaries, whether through church agencies or otherwise, Christians try to facilitate the recognition and acceptance of those values. Of course they fall short, but they don't (or shouldn't) just walk away shamefacedly; they look for ways of putting things right, and they look for ways of avoiding any repetition of their failure. Clearly this would be the response of any person of true moral worth. Nothing that the Christian faith claims about forgiveness warrants Christians settling for less.

The word 'holy' simply means 'set apart'. The Church has no other business than to promote, proclaim and celebrate the kingdom of God. Whether other people become Christians as a result is a matter for God. We might think it a very welcome event if that were to happen, but the important thing is that more people live their lives in an atmosphere marked by the values of the kingdom, and enriched because people around them are trying to live that way too.

In the word 'catholic' we find some possibilities for confusion. The word itself means simply 'universal, all-embracing'. It was introduced into the Creed in the first instance as a counter to Gnostic belief (yes, them again) that only a select few among humanity would enjoy the benefits of the gospel. 'Catholic' implies that the gospel can, and should, be made known to everyone.

There is a catholic Church based in a north-western suburb of Rome. There are other catholic churches that are less unified in structure and whose beliefs are undoubtedly very close to those of the Roman church. None of these, the Roman church included, *is* 'the holy catholic Church', which is an abstract concept. *Together* these churches embody the holy catholic Church. No part of it is complete without the others, and the relationships between these separate churches provide an opportunity for Christians to behave in the public arena in ways that are consonant with the values of the kingdom. That Christians have so often signally failed to conduct themselves in such a way is a flagrant denial of the unity of fellowship in the presence of one God.

It is possible to say, therefore, that the kingdom of God is something that we have among us now, and yet it is something that lies ahead of us in terms of human history.

There is, however, a more general idea embedded in this phrase about the holy catholic Church. It is that the life of faith is one that is lived in community. It is not just the work of the individual mind, wrestling with questions and reaching conclusions – whether provisional or final – about what to believe. Nor is it the work of the individual will as we try to identify and live by worthy standards of conduct. It is a concerted life, as we learn to accept and cherish and collaborate with a whole range of people whose views and expectations, not to mention gifts and enthusiasms, are different – sometimes markedly different – from our own.

The Church, then, is about community. It is also about reflecting the sense of transcendence which has been a pervasive theme of this book. The Church's task is to point beyond itself and its everyday concerns about buildings, staffing and money, to the transcendent God and God's message of love.

Sometimes in acknowledging that transcendent reference point, the Church has prized excellence – excellence in music, architecture, preaching, ritual, administration and more. The slogan 'Only the very best is good enough for God' has certainly served to keep many on their toes as they contribute to the life of the Church. Unfortunately, however, it has had a less happy side effect: it has sometimes resulted in a sense of 'performance elitism' in the Church, whose outcome is often a dismissive response to people who 'do their best' but whose talents fall short of excellence (at least as judged by that particular critic). It can be quite a balancing act, encouraging people to give of their best and simultaneously giving space for everyone to feel fully engaged in the life of the community.

. . . and always

'(I believe in) the communion of saints'

There is no doubt that despite the symbolic significance of the resurrection of Jesus, death has marked a shadowy boundary for Christian self-confidence. It is hard (for most of us) to find death in any way an attractive prospect. Nowhere is the mystery of time more painful than as we pass the moment of death. Time cannot flow backwards to restore the dead to life. There is for ever 'clear blue water' between them and us. Apart from the heart-rending pain of separation, and the unanswerable questions about the meaning of the life that has ended, it presents us with deep and imponderable conundrums on a larger scale. If what we do with this present life is regarded as important, what are the consequences for us if we have not heeded anyone's guidance about how to live well? For Christian believers this is especially problematic, as we discussed above under 'he descended to the dead'.

The Reformation, through which the Roman church lost its stranglehold over the people of Europe, centred in part on the relationship between the living and the dead. Is it permissible to pray for the souls of the departed? The Roman church had no problem with this idea. Under a succession of medieval Popes, however, this had been turned into a business opportunity in which, in return for financial support, the Church offered to pray, on behalf of the living, for their dead kinsfolk. Martin Luther watched in dismay as the financial aspect of this facility grew to dominate the spiritual. As a result, the separating Protestant churches have always had a real problem with the idea of praying for the dead. Even today, a Roman Catholic funeral takes the form of a Requiem Mass ('requiem' = rest), in which the focus is on prayer for the repose of the deceased; Protestant funerals, on the other hand, tend to focus on the spiritual and pastoral care of the bereaved.

This 'clear blue water' between us and those who have died has other significance too. If we really believe in the continuity of life across this mysterious boundary called death, it is puzzling to me that in some parts of the Church death has become so rigorous a division. It is almost as if the dead were somehow 'off the field of play' and unable to (or forbidden to) communicate with those still *on* the field of play – and vice versa. Perhaps this is a topic that invites review.

That said, there is a further reason for this Protestant reserve, namely the way in which some people, overwhelmed by the loss of bereavement, seek to continue in some form the normal relationship with their dead loved ones. Without straying into hair-raising scare-stories, it is of real concern that such obsessions can lead to serious mental health problems. This alone may account for Protestant reluctance to engage seriously with the communion of saints, while formally professing it as part of their credal statements.

In this clause of the Creed we are reminded that death does not separate us entirely from our departed loved ones. Indeed, we are joined with them, and with all departed believers, in 'the communion of saints'. In highly picturesque language, the New Testament speaks of the saints engaged in ceaseless worship before God's throne, of which our worship is only a faint echo.

Forgiveness

'(I believe) in the forgiveness of sins,'

This statement asserts a belief in forgiveness. Our thoughts turn naturally to the human scale of forgiveness. The point about forgiveness here is that it represents moving on from the past, closing a chapter, making a fresh start. For this, four things are essential and must all fall into place.

First, there must be recognition by both parties that things have gone wrong, that injury has been done.

Second, there must be acknowledgement of at least partial responsibility. There has to be clarity here between the offender and the offended. Both have to recognize the story of how things have gone wrong, so that both are, so to speak, in the same place. And if complete agreement on that story proves beyond reach, then there must be a way for each to acknowledge the validity of the other's story without insisting that their own is the right one.

Third, there must be a willingness to forgive and to accept forgiveness, a desire to move on. This, too, is equally important for both parties. The offender may be deeply ashamed, so ashamed that he cannot see how to rid himself of that shame. But the victim, too, may be stuck in a rut, unable to free himself from his anger and resentment towards the person who injured him. He may find it as difficult as the other person to break loose from those chains.

Fourth, there must be a readiness to put the relationship on a new footing, to make a new beginning. This is equivalent to saying that we want the relationship to work, to value what the other can bring to our life. It declares the possibility that we can be re-humanized, and that the key lies right in the heart of that relationship.

But in wounding others we have not simply disrupted a single human relationship, however precious that might be. We have torn at the very fabric of our own lives – and indeed, at a part of the whole universe of persons. In the language of our faith, we are injuring, above all else, our relationship with God. Our story is inevitably part of the greater story, and the hurt is so great that for us to acknowledge it fully would destroy us. So the burden of our breaking free and moving on falls upon God.

It is in that sense that we believe in the forgiveness of sins.

There is one more thing that must be said about forgiveness. Imagine, if you can, the situation of a parent – let's call him Martin – whose child, Jane, has been killed, either by someone's carelessness or by their deliberate action. We who look on may hope that Martin would be able to forgive the perpetrator. If that declaration of forgiveness is a long time coming, we turn away, shaking our heads in disappointment. As much as anything else, we are troubled that Martin is stuck, unable to move on.

This reaction, though understandable, may be the result of overlooking an important element in the situation. Martin has undoubtedly suffered greatly, but so has his daughter Jane. Perhaps Martin can one day, for *his own* pain and loss, come to forgive the person who caused Jane's death, but what of the injury and loss *to Jane herself*? She is not in a position to work through her experience and make for herself that journey to the place of forgiveness. Might it not be that Martin is here seeing himself as in some way the guardian or executor of Jane's interests? In refusing to forgive (whether consciously or unconsciously), Martin may be keeping alive the recognition that someone has suffered for whom no reparation is now possible at all, no apology, no healing, no opportunity to confront the perpetrator and seek reconciliation.

Society may punish the offender for the injury done to the social order, but all too often it fails to respect Jane's situation, and indeed Martin's situation as he exercises his parental responsibility towards Jane.

Forgiveness, moreover, must not displace the need for the offender to confront his (or her) own misconduct and pay a due price for it.

In declaring our belief in forgiveness, the Creed helps to remind us of what we might call a forgiveness agenda – a requirement that a way must be found through the tangle of emotional undergrowth that can so easily bar our way forward. This demands hard, not to say painful, work on both sides, both offender and victim – and, as we have seen, it draws in also anyone who is emotionally bonded to the victim in a way that entrusts to them the ongoing care of the victim's interests. Hugely daunting though this agenda is, the Creed declares that it is possible to work through it and come out on the other side. We believe in the forgiveness of sins; not simply that forgiveness is *compulsory*, but that it is *possible*, painful though the journey to it may be.

'(I believe in the) resurrection of the body'

Who am I? What is it that is you? What attributes about you could undergo change and still leave you feeling as though you were your real self? Is it your voice, your thoughts, your dreams? Are you simply the point where a hundred relationships meet? Are you, perhaps, the sight that greets you in the bathroom mirror each morning? By the amazing techniques of cosmetic surgery, the outlines of face and body can be re-drawn by surgeons to make what others see when they look at us match how we 'see' ourselves.

It's the stuff of story and film. There are several stories[1] about a person who has inexplicably woken up with a new face and, so far as the world around them was concerned, a new identity, yet who felt themself to be still themself. But no one would listen to them.

It has puzzled and traumatized people for hundreds, if not thousands of years. In the newspapers not long ago there was a piece about a man who suffered a cancer that left him with a terribly disfigured face. Yet he carried on practising law. He remained himself. He felt that the greater change took place in the people around him.

Eventually, of course, death comes: the end of life, when hearts cease to beat and flesh begins to decompose, when the voice is stilled and the thoughts can no longer be shared with another. It is here that our anxieties about our selves and our identity are most sharply focused.

It is inevitable that such reflections take us beyond the point

---

1 See, for example, the film *Face/Off* (1997), starring John Travolta and Nicolas Cage. A revolutionary medical technique allows an undercover agent to take on the physical appearance of a major criminal and infiltrate his organization.

where our words and thoughts can give us much help. It is there, for many of us, that things become interesting. In the New Testament, perhaps St Paul was the most courageous writer in tackling questions like these. Everyone around him believed that the end of all things would be soon, with Jesus returning in glory to take them all to glory. And then it didn't happen. Year after year went by, and people died (or, to use the then-popular euphemism, 'fell asleep in the Lord'). This was when the picture got really complicated. Someone had to produce answers to hard questions. So Paul got stuck in.

His answer was to use the word 'body' to be the key marker of our identity. But he wasn't talking in terms of 'Five-foot-eight, eleven-stone-six, greying hair, slight stoop, double chin'. He was talking in terms of that elusive cocktail of ingredients that makes the real you. Not biochemistry, but personality. Not dissection on a slab, but story – your story.

And Paul's conclusion was that though we shall all be changed (no more of that 'five-foot-eight' stuff), we shall still be ourselves. Charles Wesley once wrote these words: 'All shall then be lost in God.' Wonderful stuff to sing at the end of a service, but not, on reflection, one of Charles Wesley's happiest lines!

In the end, says Paul – in the end, says the gospel – all is not lost. When Jesus talks of bringing to the Father all that had been given him, he was talking about persons, not soup. The meaning of your life and mine, whether it was wretched or tranquil, will not be lost in a sea of humanity. God will welcome you as yourself.

'(I believe in) the life everlasting'

Or, as I find it in one version of the Bible: 'eternal life'.

And this immediately brings us right to the heart of the Christian faith. Earlier on in this book we mentioned 'the metaphor of time'. To stress the importance of something, set it in a story about the beginning or the end of everything. So, to explain how things are, tell a story about creation; to point to ultimate values, tell a story about the end of all things.

When we were thinking about the resurrection just now, we

were aware of the problem that beset Paul's contemporaries, who really were expecting Jesus back any time soon, and when that didn't happen they had to go back to the drawing-board and rethink the matter.

The hard question was: Is this going to happen in my lifetime, or is it something that will happen at the end of time? Certainly as a Christian I have to take account of it either way. If it will happen at the end of time, then I have to attend to what it says about the importance of this, and the trivial nature of that, in the way I live my life. If it will happen soon, then, so to speak, I'd better be looking at my passport and packing my bags.

So we come to this, the final clause of the Apostles' Creed. We believe in the life everlasting. Is this a matter of unending continuity – go on, go on, go *on*? For many discerning people, that means carrying on living with our present limitations. For me, it means never being able to play Bach's Passacaglia and Fugue in C Minor perfectly, because I haven't nearly enough talent to do it. The distinguished astronomer Sir Fred Hoyle, an agnostic, said he would find eternal life intolerable, precisely because he felt that he'd done all he could with the talents he'd been given. I can understand what he meant!

So what does eternal – or everlasting – life mean?

Let's go back to a question we raised earlier: Who am I? What is it about me that makes me *me*? What is the essence of *me*? How can that *me* take on board all that God meant me to be – which isn't about playing the perfect Bach Fugue, or cooking the perfect soufflé?

In John's Gospel we find the Christian answer to the question. Jesus talked about being born from above, which is neither more nor less than taking on board all that God meant me to be. Some have talked about this in terms of the quality of our life – the quality of the way we live, not the features of our environment.

In a sense, it is about how we can transcend our limitations as humans and as people, how we can rise above those limitations. It is about the good life – no, the *best* life. This is a question people have been asking for centuries. The Greeks of Jesus' time and three or four centuries before answered it in one way; Christians answer it in another. Members of other faith-communities will answer it their own ways. And this final affirmation of our Creed sets out our Christian conviction that such life is possible, both in principle and in reality. It is not to be dismissed as empty idealism. It can be reality for you and for me, right now.

Everlasting life, then, is not (as Sir Fred Hoyle so feared) this life extended infinitely in time. It is this life transformed into a quality that could actually measure up to being infinitely extended in time. That might mean seeing our present hopes and dreams, our ambitions and disappointments, even our limited talents and imaginations, in a new perspective.

But before we leave the Creed, let's glance forward again. Is it *now*? Or is it *not yet*? Is it something we have, or something humanity looks forward to? Well, it's both. The Methodist Communion Service includes, in one of the prayers after Communion, words about 'a foretaste of the heavenly banquet prepared for all mankind'.

So, it is both now and not yet. To quote another hymn: 'We have enough, yet not too much to long for more'.

'Amen.'

Does this simple word actually have any meaningful content? The answer, of course, is 'Yes' – and 'No'! It represents our informed assent to what has gone before. Amen: so be it! This is not merely an intellectual assent, but a whole-of-life commitment to what the words of the Creed signify.

Part 3

Believing in Context

It is time to draw the threads together. Having completed the tour of the Creed in Part 2, we need to think about a serious question: Why believe?

My answer – which may sound conceited – is that I have been committed to this faith all my life. I lay no claim to have taken it anything like as seriously as I should. No one should look to me as a model instance of a believer – or indeed as a model instance of anything else. My life has been a constant quest for answers, and an equally steadfast acceptance that answers will remain elusive. There is a vast amount that I do not understand about faith. In response to much of the Creed, I must remain silent and perplexed. Yet I can stand and say, 'I believe.'

There is a story in the Gospels about a man who brought his epileptic son to Jesus to be healed. Unfortunately Jesus was away on business – on a private and very significant walk with his three closest friends – so his other disciples tried to do what they had seen Jesus do on many occasions. They tried to heal the boy, but failed utterly. When Jesus returned, the man pleaded with him to help. Jesus responded with an astonishing statement: 'Everything is possible for those who believe.' The distraught father's reply is cherished by many who find faith hard: 'I believe; help my unbelief.' I – and many other believers – would echo that man's words.

We have examined the Context that forms the background to people's believing. We have looked at the Content of Christian believing, as we have toured the Apostles' Creed. In the course of this tour we have emphasized – gently, I hope – the possibility that there are ways of reading Bible and Creed other than to treat them as if they were instruction manuals for, say, maintaining a washing machine. I hope readers will be open to the further possibility that these 'other ways' might actually be more helpful in making the faith of the Church their own.

But we are indeed not yet done. We must turn back to the modern world – which now we should perhaps call the postmodern world – and address some of the remaining challenges that militate against believing.

As a stepping-stone on this last part of our journey, we look back over our shoulder (as it were) at the Creed, noticing that although it says much about being a Christian believer, there is much about which it says nothing at all – and this extra is in fact very important to being a Christian. Chapter 8, therefore, raises a few concerns about which the Creed is silent.

Chapter 9 takes us to the aspect of believing that most people, I suspect, find really difficult: Why does bad stuff happen to good people?

Chapter 10 takes us in a rather different direction, examining the place of believing set alongside behaving and belonging, in the attempt to answer – or at least open up – the question: Is what I believe the most important thing anyway?

Chapter 11 reviews some modern attempts to summarize the content of faith. Strictly they are not creeds at all; that term is rightly reserved for the classic ecumenical creeds of the Church. Why have these modern variants been written? In what ways do they differ from the classic ecumenical creeds of the Church? What place, if any, do they have in the life of our contemporary Church?

Chapter 12 brings our journey to an end, not by locking the door and shutting out the light, but by urging readers to continue their exploration.

8

What the Creed Does Not Say

When a committed Christian encounters the Creed, she might just feel a momentary sensation of uneasiness. It's not necessarily that the Creed is wrong in its formulations; the problem may lie not in what the Creed says, but in what it does not say. In fact there are many aspects of Christian faith about which the Creed is silent. It is our task in this part of the book to explore these gaps in the Creed's coverage.

Why the gaps? Why does the Creed leave so much unsaid? I'm not sure there is an easy answer to that question, but it may have something to do with the very different understanding, prevalent in the early Christian centuries, of how individuals relate to the Church. Then the faithful were required to assent to the creeds and attend to the sacraments of Holy Communion, Penance and so on. They were not expected to inquire further about the details and the mechanics of it all. So the Creed could be very economical, limiting its pronouncements to what really mattered in such a context.

We look first at three words – 'grace', 'covenant' and 'discipleship' – that can be very confusing because each of them has both a modern, everyday meaning and also a technical meaning. We then revisit the Bible and look at its history and main themes. Finally in this chapter we look briefly at the question of prayer.

Grace

Throughout our discussion of the Creed we have been hinting at the experience of God as 'goodness'. But sitting back and reflecting on this claim, it seems counter-intuitive. It seems to run so clearly in the face of real life as experienced by many people, the countless victims of disease, disaster, war and oppression. They are counted in billions, the world over. How is it possible to spit in the face of this *evidence* and claim that God is good?

This is a huge topic and has attracted many thinkers. I do not seek to add yet another voice to their number. Certainly I want to encourage you to regard it as an open question, one on which you should continue to read and reflect. A distinguished Methodist preacher of a couple of generations ago used to say that anyone who didn't find this question baffling was either hard in the heart or soft in the head. But in what we have said already there is the germ of a response.

We have stressed the value of the metaphorical approach, digging behind the words and the foreground ideas to identify, if possible, the core concepts that are being expressed. We have argued that this can be a more fruitful approach than the requirement to take the words literally.

In particular, when discussing phrases like 'the Father almighty, creator of heaven and earth', we tried to unpick what might be the real issues behind these rather mysterious words. We argued that these phrases have resulted from an attempt to work out logically the implications of transcendence. If God is transcendent, then God must have unchallenged authority over what happens. Indeed, God must have created everything. True, on one view this is a benign world of order and beauty, abundant in resources. But some things are altogether different, malign and hostile – at least from the point of view of human persons and communities: earthquakes, tsunamis and volcanoes, for example.

Many writers[1] have tried to address these problems from a variety of angles. To a large extent they read like the work of a diligent defence counsel working his socks off to get God acquitted of the charge of being either incompetent or wantonly cruel. This topic is known technically as 'theodicy'.

---

1 See, for example, J. Hick, *Evil and the God of Love*, London: Fontana, 1974.

D. Z. Phillips[2] concluded that the only way around this is to abandon the notion that God is omnipotent. The world is the way it is, and any alternative would be worse in a graver sense than merely counting disaster victims. The only meaningful way forward is to recognize that God is present alongside us, sharing our pain.

This is certainly helpful, because it reinforces a notion that we did discuss earlier, namely the idea that the transcendent meets us at the level of the personal – the whole person, not just the intellect or the heart, and certainly not simply at the level of ugly brute facts.

But it needs to be amplified somewhat. A key part of our thinking here is the word 'grace'. What is grace? We can try to answer this in several ways.

First, grace is unmerited generosity. God does not love us because we deserve it; God loves us simply because God loves us. God's love does not need to be justified by pointing to our unimpeachable lifestyle, our unflagging kindness to neighbours, our heroism in the face of danger, or our financial contributions to good causes. Nothing that might be found in our genes, or that we can add to our CV, will increase it or cause it to dry up.

This is quite hard to take, for the reason I have already set out: on the face of it the world is a very harsh place, and there seems to be abundant evidence that God (if there is a God) does not love us at all – or if God does love us, it is only a capricious and unreliable love! As I write this, the nation is in outrage because a little child was cruelly mistreated and died – not the first, and probably not the last. Our sense of justice is violated and it makes us angry.

There is, however, another reason why we find this idea difficult, and it is deeply embedded in our psychological history. The reason is simply stated: we have a strong belief in cause and effect; any unfolding story that doesn't demonstrate this strong link is an anomaly. Spectacular success without any preparatory hard work is an anomaly; it doesn't fit what we expect should be the case. We may respond, 'Good luck to him', but our sense of justice is disturbed. When we step back and look at our own lives,

---

2 D. Z. Phillips, *The Problem of Evil and the Problem of God*, London, SCM Press, 2004.

we have to acknowledge that many of the good things that have happened to us were not strictly down to our wisdom, or skill, or goodness; they just happened. We may say that 'We were in the right place at the right time' as an indirect way of acknowledging this element of luck in our lives. At heart, however, we see it as an anomaly. Things oughtn't to be this way (though we're not ungrateful for our own good fortune). There ought to be some connection between the way people behave and the state of their health, their relationships and their bank balance. Often there is no such connection, and it puzzles us.

So this idea of grace comes in from left field, so to speak, and breaks into our inner musings with something of a shock. We have to confess that at first it doesn't really seem to help. If God really does love us, why is it that for so very many people – like that tiny child unspeakably abused – God's love appears to have no effect at all?

Before you throw this book down in dismay (or disgust) I would remind you that many of the statements that the Bible and the Creed make are not empirical statements like 'The sun is shining'; they are instead 'value statements' about the kind of world we believe God has always wanted to see. If it isn't the way it should be, then there's something wrong with the way humanity is operating in this environment. Because we are part of humanity, we share the responsibility for a society in which a child can die through abuse and neglect, just as we share responsibility for proxy wars on a distant continent whose national boundaries were drawn by our own ancestors for their own convenience and with little thought for the realities of the existing tribal order.

Our own experience of grace prompts us to do our utmost to promote the idea that our human world should operate according to the transcendent values of God's love, which is undivided, undeflected by the choices humans have made. We are assured that our orientation is the same as God's orientation – towards the flourishing of life. Grace is not coercive; it leaves us in control, carrying responsibility for playing our part in the fullness of Life.

This notion of grace encapsulates the idea that the transcendent is *listening to* us and *addressing* us and *providing for* us in love. Central to this is the idea that this flow of love (or, if you prefer, goodwill) has nothing to do with our deserving it. In short, we are not in competition with one another for God's love.

The problem with competition, in the world of business, is that it is often seen as a zero-sum game. If one business is successful, we may suppose, then another business must fail precisely because of its rival's success. Perhaps it is this that gives competition a bad name. But the disadvantages of monopoly are well understood in the world of business. Business leaders actually relish competition and do not seek the slack and dissolute world of the monopoly.

Alfie Kohn[3] has pointed out the dangers of a rampantly competitive culture. First published in 1986, his book has been provoking comment ever since. Kohn argues that our society's preference for competition over against co-operation is profoundly destructive – destructive of our health and of the well-being of our society. Kohn's subsequent work has been particularly critical of styles and patterns of education that seek to privilege competition over co-operation. Such patterns, he argues, prevent the development of team-working; they inhibit trust, and therefore they militate against the very business success which they claim as their goal.

It is interesting to reflect on a related phenomenon in the development of Christian theology: the doctrine of election – the idea that God's choice has precedence over our virtue or our vice in determining our ultimate fate. Perhaps its most noted advocate was Jean Calvin, the Genevan reformer. As a theological idea, election has suffered from two major confusions. The first is its link with predestination, which has led many to suppose that their fate is sealed and has nothing whatever to do with their practical conduct during their lifetime; there is neither purpose nor need to behave well. The second confusion arises from the misunderstanding that election – with its emphasis on God's choice – implies that God has, from the very beginning of time, chosen a few to 'inherit the kingdom' and many to suffer permanent exclusion from it. In other words, election implies choice, and God's choice of some implies rejection of others. In fact, the point of the doctrine of election was quite the reverse. Its aim was to make unequivocally clear the idea that our status before God depends

3 A. Kohn, *No Contest: The Case Against Competition*, Boston, Houghton Mifflin, 1992.

simply and solely on God's love; our feeble attempts at virtue cannot guarantee God's favour, nor can our calamitous vices ultimately frustrate God's loving purpose – that would make God's love dependent upon human behaviour rather than upon the love which is inherent in God's nature.

This is most concisely expressed in the phrase that has become almost a meaningless cliché: God is love.

Covenant

In Chapter 5, on God, we looked at the idea that the transcendent might – and indeed does – become apparent to us in relational terms. That is, we grasp the transcendent through those faculties within our humanity which are closely linked with the person we are. In short, our knowledge of God, such as it is, is personal rather than intellectual.

The notion of covenant appears in several places in the biblical tradition. In the Old Testament, there are covenants between God and Noah, God and Abraham (several times), God and Jacob. Later there are strong hints that this process of covenant-making is not over. Jeremiah and Ezekiel talk about covenants on a new basis. Whereas the earlier covenants took a form that resembled a legal contract ('You do this for me and I'll do that for you'), this new covenant would take the form of an inner transformation, a profound change of heart, rather than be embodied in a document that can be filed away and referred to or forgotten. We might sum this up in the phrase: 'I *am* for you.' From God to humans, this implies an unswerving love; from humans to God, it implies a devotion to God-the-transcendent that involves the whole of our being.

In the New Testament, of course there is a New Covenant – perhaps the writers of the New Testament (and, of course, perhaps Jesus himself) envisaged this New Covenant as being the realization of the new covenants that were promised in the writings of Jeremiah and Ezekiel.

The central element in this New Covenant is that there is now the possibility of a qualitatively new relationship between God and God's people (plural, in that it refers to communities) and God's people (singular, in that it is offered to individuals who must respond as individuals).

In describing this New Covenant, the writers of the New Testament deployed concepts and mechanisms that were deeply grounded in their Jewish tradition. In particular, they made much of the notion that a covenant needed to be sealed in blood to indicate beyond doubt that the signatories took it and the attendant obligations with the utmost seriousness.

We have been thinking about the creeds as metaphors – apparently concrete statements that carry a hidden meaning that couldn't be communicated by any other means. We have been trying to unpack those metaphors to see whether we could describe what lay behind them in more accessible modern language.

So what lies behind the notion of covenant?

One of the most striking metaphors in the Bible is the way in which intimate human relationships are used as metaphors for the human–divine relationship. In our marriage services we are reminded of this, likening the bond between marriage partners to that between Christ and his Church.

The Old Testament writers stick to this metaphor when they want to castigate the people of God for abandoning this central relationship in their community life – the relationship with God. At several points in their history their commitment to Yahweh, their ancestral god, wavers; they dally with the gods worshipped by their foreign neighbours, sometimes because it's more fun, and makes less serious demands upon them! The prophets liken such behaviour to reckless and wilful promiscuity. The language they use is unrestrained, almost sickening to a modern mind. Yet those ancient prophets felt that nothing less dramatic and vivid would express their utter repugnance at such behaviour.

More and more frequently in our modern world we are finding examples of what is sometimes called 'commitment phobia'. The increasing trends towards marriage breakup – or towards forms of relationship that don't carry the possibility or the stigma of divorce – all suggest that commitment is unfashionable. It involves, after all, handing over control of part of your life to some objective or purpose or person. There is also an increasing reluctance for people to get involved in ways that require the sacrifice of time and energy. Youth clubs and uniformed organizations founder because there aren't enough adults willing to make the commitment to stick with it, come what may.

A sociological analysis of this phenomenon is outside the scope of our present discussion. It may have something to do with increasing demands of the world of work, fuelled in turn by the need to operate in a global marketplace. It may have something to do with the need, felt by many young families, for both parents to undertake a heavy work-commitment in order to fund the purchase of a house. So, arguably, the dearth of youth leaders is not necessarily a failure of commitment as such; it may be simply that life involves too much commitment already and people are unable to sustain voluntary commitments over and above the absolutely necessary ones. And all too often, people find those absolutely necessary commitments unsustainable – hence the rising numbers of single-parent families.

There may be many responses to this situation, for the entire voluntary sector, including churches. It is not our place here to work out those issues in great depth. Rather, we may be able to point out the biblical concept of covenant as a marker of commitment and a signal that commitment is important.

From the notion of the transcendent we may derive certain values by which to order our own lives and the life of our community. The way we apply those values indiscriminately for the good of others as well as for our own strictly personal interest, is a measure of our covenant commitment to the transcendent – to God, in fact. Relationships of all kinds, from the intimate trust between husband and wife (or same-sex partners, don't forget), through loyalties to the team and to the employer, are potentially examples of covenant relationships. Increasingly, however, and despite legislation to counter this trend, they have assumed the character of time-limited contractual relationships; the employee has become a business partner with whom commitment is strictly limited – a unit of labour; a commodity.

There is in this idea of covenant something else which is important: the idea of accountability. When people talk about accountability they often mean accountability for other people

– i.e. that other people must be accountable for their mistakes ('Heads must roll'). Within the Church I find that people actually want accountability, simply to know whether they are doing what people want them to do. I admit that my experience of the world of work is very limited (I spent all my adult life in one kind of paid employment, that of university teacher), so I wouldn't want anyone to suppose that in my opinion the Church is unique. But it is possible, isn't it, that people in the Church seek accountability because their roles are very diffuse and ill-defined? How do I know if I'm succeeding if there's nothing for me to measure? And once again, this notion of covenant brings us back to the framework of relationship which is, in the end, the most complete form of accountability.

We end this brief account of the idea of covenant by musing on the idea that we have a relationship with God. At first blush it seems quite absurd – if we are to believe what theologians tell us about the transcendence of God. Yet when I told my atheist colleague that I felt a sense of being addressed, her response – understandably guarded but far from dismissive – appeared to admit the idea to thoughtful circles.

When, in my youth, I followed a course of preparation for becoming a church member, we used a document called 'The Senior Catechism of the Methodist Church'. It was typical of one tradition of bringing young people into the life of the Church – a sort of question-and-answer tour of what Christians need to believe and understand. The first question, as I recall it, was this:

> Q: What is the chief end of man?
> A: The chief end of man is to know God and enjoy Him (*sic*) for ever.

It wasn't exactly user-friendly. But this definition did introduce an important idea, namely that our relationship with God is one to be *enjoyed*. This is not a frivolous invitation to do what you like. Rather, it is a claim that this relationship should bring us a sense of joy like no other; it should nourish our inner being as nothing else can. So, one view of this covenant is that God's intention is that (in the words of the Catechism) we should *enjoy* him. Discipleship is partly about *learning to enjoy God*. This in turn implies taking time for that learning process to reach its full flower.

But if our dealings with God are indeed a relationship, then doesn't it make sense to set our imaginations to work on the question: What does this relationship feel like from God's end? And one question that arises immediately is: If enjoyment can be a part of the deal from our end, can it also be part of the deal from God's end too? So, another aspect of discipleship is *learning to live so that God can enjoy us*. And that is indeed a lifetime's work.

Perhaps in these missing elements of the Creed we may find things worth saying to the contemporary world.

Discipleship

The Creed, as we have seen, is composed of a series of propositions, or truth-claims. It invites us to assent to those truth-claims. But also, and we have stressed this too, the first affirmation of the Creed – '*I believe*' – sets out our claim to an identity. Three words have recurred throughout this book: behaving, believing and belonging. We have given by far the greatest attention to believing, a little to belonging, and hardly any to behaving. In the section on the holy catholic Church we have seen how important it is that we learn to live in community. By this we do not mean a commune, living together 24/7. Yet the Church is not a grouping that we associate with simply because it suits us. As David Harned puts it: 'The self exercises its choice as it does only because it has first been chosen.'[4] A church, therefore, is more than a single-interest sports or hobby club. We do many things together. But above all we share our journey of discipleship together. We are called (chosen) to support one another in that journey.

The Creed underpins that shared journey, providing us with words and phrases that remind us of what we are committed to. It is that shared commitment to God in Christ, which we have avowed in saying the Creed, which provides us with our identity. The Creed does not, therefore, need to go into detail about

4 D. B. Harned, *Creed and Personal Identity: The Meaning of the Apostles' Creed*, Philadelphia, Fortress Press, 1981.

the *how* of discipleship. The Creed implies discipleship, for we cannot say the Creed without involving ourselves in the journey of discipleship.

We found, earlier on in our journey, that believing in Jesus implies a personal commitment to working out what it might mean to follow Jesus (= putting our faith in his way of doing things) in every aspect of our lives. This brings us into the company of those who are trying to follow him: his disciples.

People join churches for many reasons, which fall roughly into the areas of *believing* (because the belief-system helps us to make sense of life) or *belonging* (because the friendship and support of the church community has enabled us to surmount a personal crisis). People remain in church because of shared values and mutual commitment – adding the *behaving* component.

The religious concept of discipleship has a number of modern correlates. We might think of a group of graduate students working with a senior researcher; a group of athletes working with a very experienced coach; or a group of traumatized people working in an encounter group with an experienced facilitator. Such images bring out the central idea of following someone, accepting guidance from someone.

Another area of modern life which may offer illuminating parallels is the idea of professional formation, in which an aspiring individual is guided through a series of experiences designed to form good habits of thought and of work, to teach the necessary theoretical foundations and practical skills, to adopt high standards of conduct and practice, and to ensure that such attitudes are widespread through the profession (whatever that profession may be). In parallel with, and perhaps related to, the pursuit of excellence which we mentioned earlier, the phrase 'Continuing Professional Development' has come to the fore as an element of our working lives. Many organizations have adopted it either by defining it or by setting out a programme of activity which ensures that it happens. Here is a definition found on the website of the Training and Development Agency for Schools:

> Continuing professional development (CPD) consists of reflective activity designed to improve an individual's attributes,

knowledge, understanding and skills. It supports individual needs and improves professional practice.

To be effective, CPD should be directly relevant to the participants, clearly identify intended outcomes, take account of previous knowledge and expertise, model effective teaching and learning strategies, and include impact evaluation designed as part of the activity from the outset.

In contrast, the website of the Law Society provides[5] only a comprehensive list of courses and other activities, together with a programme setting out how an individual member can make the best possible use of these facilities for their personal and professional development.

In Christian terms, the notion of discipleship shares much with these secular models. It involves following a master, acquiring skills and theoretical understanding, adopting a mindset of high standards, learning the arts of planning what is to be done in accordance with professional standards and principles, and later, reflection on what has happened with the objective of augmenting the body of knowledge and skill.

Is there not, however, a profound difference between being a professional (accountant or lawyer, doctor or teacher) and being a Christian? After all, professional development relates to competence and quality of performance in the professional sphere. Being a Christian touches the whole of life; there is no moment when you are not a Christian.

Against that, it can be argued that some professional bodies have a Code of Conduct as well as a Code of Practice. The Code of Practice is about the standards expected of the professional in the strictly technical aspects of her work, whereas the Code of Conduct refers to the ethical standards expected in dealings with clients, colleagues and the general public, including the very broad requirement to uphold the reputation of the profession. In short, the Code of Practice is about competence, the Code of Conduct is about probity. We may say, then, that although the Code of Conduct addresses broader issues than the Code of Practice, it

5 Both these web-searches were carried out in mid-2008; it is of course likely that the two websites referred to here have now changed.

still relates to a specific area of life – loosely the work-related area. The distinction between being a professional and being a Christian is therefore a valid one, though we may learn a good deal from the fruitful interplay of ideas between the two.

There is, however, in all good teaching, whatever the area of knowledge or skill concerned, an element which is the emulation of a respected practitioner. In Christian terms this is clearly seen in the account of Jesus calling a group of 12 people 'to be with him' (Mark 3.13). The consequences for the person who is attempting to 'follow Jesus' are considerable. Whereas the Creed-culture suggests it's all a matter of believing (and that in an intellectual, propositional sense), discipleship covers a much wider territory. It includes the ways in which we react towards other people, our awareness of the wider world around us, the way we use our time and talents, the atmosphere we breathe (as a metaphor for the ideas we entertain and cultivate). Lest anyone should think this adds up to a total takeover of personality, it does not amount to a set of general dictatorial rules robbing us of freedom with regard to our tastes in music, literature, the arts, holidays, education, finances and so on. Quite possibly these will be affected by our discipleship, but what is quite certain is that there is no campaign systematically to extinguish our personality.

The Bible

One of the strangest omissions from the Creed – not least because of its central position in the recent history of Christian discipleship – is the Bible itself.

We need to make two points here. First, the creeds were composed in an era when literacy was confined to a very few people indeed. As a result, the position of Bible reading in Christian discipleship was not a major issue at all until the invention of the printed book, and its consequence – the wider spread of literacy. Christians sometimes talk of being 'people of the book' and see in that a point of commonality with Jews and Muslims. While that may be at least partly true (though these three religious traditions do view their scriptures rather differently), what is certain is that only in the last four or five centuries has the Bible become a 'book of the people'. In earlier times there was no expectation of new Christians that they would be regular personal students of the Bible. There was no need, therefore, for the credal confessions to refer to the place of scripture in being a Christian.

The second point is that the composition and compilation of the collection of diverse literary works known collectively to Christians as the Holy Bible took place over a long period of time. They were subject to a great deal of editorial revision and refinement, to meet the needs of communities scattered over the known world, over a long historical time-chart, and facing hugely differing social circumstances. In many ways the Bible can be described as the product of the Church – and before it, of the Jewish communities that produced, nurtured and preserved the books of the Hebrew Bible, which Christians inherit as the Old Testament. In saying this, of course, we are not seeking to diminish in any way the role of divine or transcendent inspiration in its content. A clear distinction needs to be drawn, however, between on the one hand claiming that the text of the Bible was dictated to its human authors by some divine agency and written, preserved and translated across the centuries in an essentially accurate state, and on the other reading it as simply the product of human social conditions. We might regard these two claims as corresponding to positions 2 and 1 in our opening discussion, right back in Chapter 2. As you might expect, I would want to stake out a position somewhere between these two. Inspiration, yes! Dictation, no!

We read the Bible because it gives us a sense of belonging, a sense of sharing in the lives of communities long past – their struggles and their triumphs, their insights and their tragic mistakes, their experiences of being addressed, and their experiences of faithful expectant prayer that was met with silence.

The book of Genesis, right at the beginning of the Bible, has been read in many ways. A Jewish scholar, Aviva Gottlieb Zornberg, daughter of an Orthodox Rabbi and a professional psychotherapist, has written a marvellous book, *Genesis: The Beginning of Desire*,[6] in which she probes the possible mental states of the

6 A. G. Zornberg, *Genesis: The Beginning of Desire*, Philadelphia, Jewish Publication Society, 1995.

patriarchs as they faced one challenge after another. Illuminating and deeply challenging, this book adds one more thread to the catalogue of ways of entering into the life of the Bible.

It is a mistake to look in the Bible for a historical record in the sense that a modern historian might hope to create through her researches. That was not its purpose; indeed, most ancient people would have been baffled by our modern notions of scientific history. As we have remarked before, what matters is the meaning, and if in order to make the meaning clear we have to adjust the story somewhat, so be it.

Many themes can be found in the Bible, though this is not the place to explore all of them. One theme that is relevant to our present discussion comes across with great clarity. We have spoken briefly of the sense of being addressed. This awareness is found in so many biblical stories that it is a clear motif of the biblical tradition. On page after page we read of the Lord (God) speaking – though it is far from clear how this sensation was perceived by those who reported it.

This sense of being addressed goes beyond a sense of awe and mystery, which may arise in many ways: a walk through a beech wood in early spring, a glimpse of a kingfisher under overhanging willow trees, sunlight falling on the contours of a hillside sculpted long ago by glacial action, a child's first hesitant steps, a piece of music. This sense of being addressed engages not merely one's emotions but one's whole self. For Christian believers it arises in the practice of praying – not emailing God with our shopping list of things we'd like to happen, but waiting in patient silence for a resonance between ourselves and the transcendent.

I am conscious that here we are employing a metaphor, simply because there is no other way of describing what happens. It would be interesting to explore this metaphorical relationship between meditation, being addressed and resonance, but that is not the object of this present discussion. For Christian believers, the Bible is often a valuable prompt and guide for that meditation, as well as being a reminder that one outcome of meditation is this sense that the presence of God, this resonance, or whatever we want to call it, has in some way clarified things for us.

A recurring theme of this book has been 'the big picture', the transcendent. This working principle can be applied also to the way in which we read and use the Bible. There is a big picture, an overarching thread in the Bible. When we draw information from the particular details, we must be aware of that big picture. For Christians, not surprisingly, the life and ministry of Jesus is the key to a Christian way of reading the Bible. Some would go so far as to say (as Marcion did in the second century) that the Old Testament is useless because anything said in it which is consistent with the teaching of Jesus is now unnecessary, and everything else is worthless because it is wrong. The Church rightly rejected Marcion's harsh view of the Old Testament. Instead of dismissing it, the Church adopted a variety of strategies for making sense of the Old Testament as foreshadowing the events of the New. Incidentally, these strategies did not include a literal reading of the events of the Old Testament – that approach to the Bible is in fact one that dates from much more recently in the Christian era. In the twenty-first century we might adopt yet another approach. Might we not rather say: here is a part of the Jewish tradition that helps us to express the meaning of the life and ministry of Jesus?

But what exactly are we to do with the Bible? Given what we have said, for a person simply to pick it up and read it holds real danger of misunderstanding it. Before the invention of moveable type, and the subsequent expansion of literacy, ordinary Christians were not expected to read the Bible at all; they were expected to depend on the interpretations of their educated priests, who would tell them all they needed to know in a form approved by Holy Church.

The Church has come to understand that the revolution in literacy cannot be unravelled, and that in her teaching ministry she must provide Christians with the means to make good sense of what they read in the Bible. Given the wide variety of traditions within the Christian family, it is not surprising that these means do not all paint exactly the same picture in detail. The thoughtful Christian will do well to sample a number of approaches and settle on one that is helpful to her. Later on, it would be good to study material coming from a different part of the Christian family – not so she can understand how very wrong *they* are, but so she can grasp a little of the unfathomable mystery that is God. For no one has the whole truth; we are all learners.

Prayer

Prayer is in truth an enormous subject – as witness the many books that have been written about it. Writers have offered guidance about when and where to pray, how to pray, what to pray about, the elements of prayer (adoration, confession, intercession, etc.).

Perhaps the best guidance on prayer that I have ever come across I found in a little book on prayer by the late Russian Orthodox Archbishop, Metropolitan Anthony of Sourozh. He tells how, as a young and very inexperienced priest, he was approached by an old lady who asked him for some advice on prayer. Immediately he felt himself to be unprepared and inadequate for the task, but he had to say something. This is what he told his parishioner.

Go to your room, turn off the radio and television, and sit quietly doing something you enjoy doing but which doesn't take up all your mental energy. Carry on with this until you become aware of a presence in the room with you. That is the Lord. When you feel comfortable with that presence, speak with him about anything at all. When you have exhausted all you want to say, just listen and enjoy the presence.

In all honesty I cannot vouch for the total accuracy of my account here, because I no longer have the book. But the sense of the story is right. The lady went away, somewhat to Father Anthony's relief, and he thought no more about it. A few days later, however, the lady reappeared, overjoyed at the experience that had changed her life. She attributed it to the profound, wise insight of the young priest. He learned more than she did from that encounter!

Many Christians maintain a list of the people for whom they pray. They use prayer manuals (the Methodist Church publishes an excellent one every year) to remind them of the issues of concern in the worldwide Church. Many churches and church groups hold prayer meetings, the underlying theme of which is to pray *for something*; it may be an urgent decision that the church has to confront – perhaps a facet of the church's life needs additional resource; it may be a prayer for renewed vitality and vigour in the whole life of the church.

All this encourages the belief that prayer is primarily about praying for something – asking God for something. This leads very easily into a caricature of God as 'Mister Fixit', and prayer as a sort of celestial vending machine dispensing goodies of various kinds.

Underlying Father Anthony's story, however, is the most serious truth about prayer: prayer is first and foremost about giving God (the transcendent, the sacred) our serious, loving and undivided attention. We have seen that God becomes apparent in our life as one who addresses us. It follows that the life of discipleship is centrally about relationship with that one. Given that it is a relationship, it is appropriate that we should give to that relationship a level of serious attention at least comparable with that we give to any human relationship that we really value.

The teaching of Jesus on prayer – in entire harmony with the rest of the Bible, incidentally – certainly includes an element of asking for things. Jesus urges us to be persistent, not because we are like children in a toy shop before Christmas, but because we are being honest with God about the things that really matter to us. Like that lady who came to value the advice of Father Anthony, prayer is indeed the way in which God invites us to be open and upfront about what we understand our needs to be. But the second part of Father Anthony's advice was to listen. This is what we neglect. Even when we don't neglect it, we misunderstand it and leap into ill-considered action the moment we think God has given us a clear directive. What matters is the relationship – not primarily the things that are worrying us that we'd like God to fix, not primarily the things we imagine God is telling us to do, but our relationship with God. Given serious attention over the course of a lifetime, the consequences can be astonishing and transforming of lives and communities. But even then, what matters is the relationship.

9

When Things Go Wrong: Blaming and Forgiving God

In the lives of most people there are moments – occasional for some, frequent for others – when it feels as though the sky has fallen in. A relationship falls apart, investments fail, a teenager becomes involved with the police, the family breadwinner is made redundant, terminal illness is diagnosed. Everything is going wrong and everyone seems to be against us. Without any doubt these are tough times, and prompt phrases like 'The stiff upper lip', 'When the going gets tough the tough get going', and 'It'll be fine if we all pull together' – and of course, questions like 'Why me?' Most people have a strategy for trying to cope with disasters like these, at the level of carrying on functioning as a human being.

For people who believe in God, this is no less tough than for those who don't.[1] There may even be a sense in which it is tougher, if the God we believe in is like the one I have tried to describe in this book, known to us as the God of love. Why is this? Partly it is precisely because this belief (faith, trust) has been so central to the way we function as human beings. Because the bleak news challenges the foundation of our faith, it challenges us also at the level of who we are and how we function. It undermines our every attempt to formulate a coping strategy because it challenges so fundamentally the way we understand the world and ourselves in relation to it.

1 We have a little about this already in the previous chapter, under the heading 'Grace'.

Of course it is equally devastating for people whose belief is centred on the goodness or reliability of human nature. In the Bible there are many stories and poems that describe how this felt to the human writers and the communities for whom they wrote. Because they believed that God created and sustains everything, and that God had chosen, guided and protected his people, it must have felt terrible when things went badly wrong. If God is ultimately responsible for everything, then God must have decided that this should happen. It feels as though God is angry with me (or with us). But we (I) don't believe that God is cruel or capricious.

This tended to produce one basic reaction: to misquote a song from a musical, 'somewhere in our youth or childhood we must have done something bad'. So, we must apologize to God, make amends, and try to do better. In some situations this response may be appropriate, if the misfortune can be tracked back to a selfish or rash decision that we've made. But it isn't appropriate if we can't identify something we have done wrong that might account for the misfortune. It just feels like God is angry.

In an aside during a sermon on forgiveness, I asked whether people were prepared to forgive God. Afterwards I was gently taken to task by one faithful and thoughtful church member, who was clearly very puzzled by such an idea.

The theology goes like this. We believe that God created everything. Initially this was a way of declaring Yahweh to be the creator even of the other gods, who in comparison with Yahweh were therefore 'mere nothings'. This provided a convenient mental picture through which the people of Judah/Israel could remind themselves that God/Yahweh transcends absolutely everything. Like many positives, however, this contained the seeds of a negative. If God *created* everything, then God is *responsible for* everything, good and bad. And so we have a choice. On the one hand we might subscribe to a 'theology of one', in which case we must ascribe everything, good and bad, to the one God; on the other hand we might subscribe to a 'theology of two', one of whom is responsible for all the good stuff and none of the bad, and the other responsible for everything bad and nothing good. Somehow we tend also to mix up these two theologies in our heads, working with first one, then the other as it suits our mood and purpose.

The theology of two (sometimes called dualism) has some advantages for us. It allows us to believe in a God of love, and set aside the challenges of misfortune and wickedness, dumping them on another doorstep. God is not to blame for our misfortune; in the words of one of Jesus' parables, 'an enemy has done this'. The mental picture we have is one in which the world outside us is a world at war, a war between good and evil; our misfortunes are the result either of enemy action, or else of us being caught in the cross-fire. Unfortunately this belief has a number of side effects, mental habits into which we may slip unintentionally.

This picture of spiritual (or metaphysical) warfare somehow allows us to excuse ourselves from personal responsibility for our own wrongdoing. Talk of 'demon possession' can take many forms, not all of which are intensely dramatic. In its most insidious form it comes close to what St Paul described when he confessed that (my paraphrase) 'the good that I want to do I find myself incapable of; what I actually do is the evil I know I should not do' (Rom. 7.19). Paul was honest enough to acknowledge that he himself was the source of that wrongdoing that caused him so much wretchedness. He just didn't know what to do about it. The insidious form of this theology of two arises when we use it to shrug off our personal responsibility for doing something wrong, and turn it into a matter of the state of our souls.

The second side effect of the theology of two is played out on a much larger canvas. It gives legitimacy to the idea that some human groups actually embody good while others embody evil. It allows us – literally – to demonize the enemy, to regard him as sub-human; it allows us to exterminate him without the usual restraints of human respect. All war tends to become total war; all enemies tend to be cast as unremittingly evil. The popular writer Sir Terry Pratchett was once asked for his views on the saga *The Lord of the Rings*. He was disturbed, he said, by the way in which an entire race (the Orcs) was depicted as totally and entirely evil, capable of no good whatever. Global conflict, he observed, is too often painted as combat against an 'evil empire' or an 'axis of evil'.

A third side effect is similar to the second but on a slightly smaller scale. It characterizes particular groups as evil, deserving only ostracism and jeering; mental, emotional and even physical abuse against these groups is condoned and even tacitly encouraged. Ethical views are treated as absolute laws, and people who do not see things the same way are, like national enemies, regarded as sub-human and therefore outside the protection of the law. Obvious examples are lesbians and particularly gay men, medical staff who carry out abortions (even within the law), and people who carry out medical research using animals as experimental subjects. This all arises because the theology of two, technically known as dualism, justifies these human attitudes.

What about the theology of one, which is quite clearly the biblical theology ('The Lord your God is one')? Its advantages rest in its simplicity. Physicists have long searched for a unified theory of everything. We must not allow ourselves to be confused here, but there is a sense in which the theology of one is indeed a unified theory of everything (though not in the sense in which this idea is used by physicists). It leaves us, however, with a problem. According to Genesis 1, God pronounced this world good – not just in general terms but in detail, stage by stage, 'day' by 'day'. This world is found to contain evil. We need to examine what we mean by 'evil'.

One way in which people use the word 'evil' is to say of something that it is harmful to humans. We may apply this usage, for example, to diseases like cancer, malaria, tuberculosis and AIDS, as well as hunger, ignorance and natural disasters such as floods, earthquakes, droughts (though many of these usually take their toll indirectly through hunger).

It is perhaps too easy for us to treat these issues as academic or technical, remote from our everyday lives. But such a position cannot be sustained; these things leap off the pages of newspapers with heart-rending vividness. A child is born with a condition that will ensure for him a life that is short and filled with pain. After 11 years of constant love and care he dies, leaving his parents and siblings bereft and desperately sad. The question arises: Why?

We sometimes find it convenient to treat these harmful things as though they were moral evils. They are not; they are simply the result of the way in which the world of nature works. Life, for example, works through the action of proteins. The very simplest animals and plants make proteins out of the chemicals around them, using the energy of sunlight (or, in the case of some creatures in the deep oceans, energy from hot-air vents at the mid-ocean ridges). More highly developed organisms need to use proteins faster than they could synthesize them, so they commandeer proteins that other organisms have made – by eating those organisms. In the simplest case, these 'other organisms' are plants. The so-called higher animals grab their protein supplies not from plants but from other animals. This process of acquiring proteins by taking advantage of the work of other organisms is an essential part of the whole tapestry of life. It's no use calling it 'evil' in the moral sense.

Having said all that, the harmful things I listed above are not all on the same level. Let me give two examples. Ignorance is harmful because it may cause people to do things that are harmful to themselves – like drinking contaminated water. (It has to be acknowledged, of course, that millions of people drink contaminated water not out of ignorance, but because they do not have access to clean water.) But ignorance is also harmful because it gives rise to harmful consequences for others. When de-forestation weakens the structure of soil on hillsides in India, those hillsides lose their capacity for retaining water. The water rushes down to the plains and causes flooding.

This chain of causation, though not itself built of moral evils, rests nonetheless on the moral evils of ignorance and greed. The logging companies may be ignorant of the consequences of their trade; the consequences may be disastrous, but the logging companies are not, at this point, morally culpable. If, however, when that ignorance is dispelled, when they know and understand how they are the cause of others' misfortune, they continue to pursue their trade unchecked, then in their greed they are brushing aside the needs of the inhabitants of the plain. Ironically, it was the plain-dwellers who produced the food which nourished the loggers! My point is that while the evils in this list are not directly moral evils, moral evil arises nevertheless if, even with greater understanding, humans still behave in ways that result in harm to each other.

My second example concerns the human suffering that follows a volcanic eruption. One possible response to this is to shake our heads and point out the folly of living so close to a volcano. Yet it is precisely because the volcano is there and is active that the surrounding land is relatively fertile. The people may have had no choice.

A second way in which we use the word 'evil' is to denote truly moral evil, such as the deliberate abuse or exploitation of persons. In recent times there have been many examples of this, both on the large and the small scale: genocide and appalling child abuse. This leaves us with mixed feelings of horror, anger and deep sadness. How can people treat other people like this? What is the explanation for it? What can we do about it? It is at this point, perhaps, that many will shake their heads and say: 'That does it for me; I can't make sense of a God of love in the face of these horrors.' And believers too must shake their heads, sharing that sense of horror.

A third way in which we use the word 'evil' refers to human carelessness or recklessness. A worker using an industrial machine is nominally protected by safety equipment, but the safety equipment is poorly designed and uncomfortable so the worker is reluctant to use it. In an attempt to increase productivity, the worker is paid according to his or her actual output of completed work; using the safety equipment slows him down, so he is paid less. He therefore ignores the safety rules, an accident takes place and he is injured.

Here is a man who travels on the road a great deal, but is increasingly expected to maintain contact with his company. He is not, however, provided with a legal hands-free device for using his telephone (relatively) safely while driving. He switches off his phone in compliance with the law, and is reprimanded for being out of touch. Later he takes a call while driving and his distraction causes a fatal accident.

A young man seeks thrills from driving a car. He has been involved in a road traffic offence already, and has been disqualified from driving. He has no insurance. After an evening of drinking with his mates, he steals a car and indulges his favourite adrenalin-rush – driving the car at speed. Another fatal accident ensues, which he (and others) may or may not survive.

In these instances the person who has died has relatives who love him or her. Their loss is, first and foremost, that of a loved one who meant so much to them, but they are challenged by the need to accept that their loved one has deliberately done wrong.

Our Western culture tends not to be fatalistic; it does not mildly accept whatever fate doles out to us. If things go wrong, we want someone to blame, we want a head (or heads) to roll. It is almost as if comfort is believed to be a right, and if we don't find ourselves in a comfortable place, we look for someone to carry the can.

This sentiment is a worthy one for at least two reasons. It provides a motivation to get things sorted, to make 'the system' work better for people. It holds accountability to be important; if we are negligent and someone suffers, then we are held to account and will have to face the consequences.

Unfortunately, the second of these has another side to it – the assumption that a problem is solved if only we have found someone to hold accountable for failure. Solving the problem, in terms of corrective action, is never that simple. While there are certainly good grounds for punishing those whose negligence or poor judgement has resulted in tragedy, there are some situations in which a better view, surely, is that the one who has failed once is the most likely to understand how important it is not to repeat the same mistake.

We must remember that question: Why does bad stuff happen to good people? In earlier chapters we have explored some possible theological responses to this problem. We have to admit, however, that perfect answers to this question are simply not available – at least in the terms that most people would regard as satisfactory. The great mysteries of life are indeed mysteries. We do not have ready answers to them. We have to assume that the world is indeed, on the face of it, a capricious and amoral place, and we deceive ourselves if we imagine otherwise. In response, we have two choices before us. One is to assume further that our attempts to read meaning into this chaotic and miserable world are completely futile. The other is to assume instead that the presence of the transcendent is always at our side as we wrestle with the chaos and misery – not merely as intellectual conundrums, of course, but as painful realities.

10

Belonging and Behaving

We sometimes use the word 'story' to talk about (among other things) the journey of faith for an individual Christian. The story of our church community is in part the sum of the stories of each one of us. Without our individual stories the community would have only a thin story of its own. Yet for many of us, it is hard to think of our own story at all. 'I'm such an insignificant person, really, you know!' The mission and ministry of the Church is about nurturing our individual stories, enabling us to see in those stories God's tender care for us, God's encouragement to us to live as fully as we can for the benefit of all, including ourselves.

In simple terms an individual's Christian story might run something like this: life is confused, muddled, doesn't make sense, has no point; in Christ we discover afresh the aim and purpose of life, and our feet are set on a good pathway. God has set us right.

That is a possible 'model' story for you to explore and compare with your own (your very own 'myth'). But in fact there are as many stories as there are Christians, and they vary greatly. Furthermore, each journey has many steps, and the view is different at each step. After all, and especially if life is stressful or meaningless, we can be so caught up in 'where we are' that to understand, even imagine, the possibility of being 'somewhere else' on this or some other journey is impossibly difficult. It takes all of our energy to be 'where we are'.

We might think about this great variety of individual stories in this way. Here are three words: 'behaving', 'believing' and 'belonging'. In our earlier discussion on this topic, in Chapter 4, we added to our three 'b' words one more: 'becoming'. Everyone's story involves all of these words to some degree, but for each Christian's story, at a given moment, one of these words dominates.

First, the word 'behaving'. From time to time we read a book about people who have behaved in a truly dreadful way, bringing ruin to their own lives, and to the lives of others. They reach a 'low point' of real desperation, and feel deeply guilty about what they have done to other people and the waste they have made of their own lives. By chance (it seems) they encounter the Christian story – perhaps they pick up a Bible and read it, or a real person comes alongside them and tells them about Jesus. Gradually, or perhaps suddenly, everything clicks into place and they are able to make a dramatic fresh start. Their behaviour is changed. Their life is re-built around Jesus. They have identified with the Jesus story in a way that mirrors Jesus' identification with humanity.

Stories like this are wonderfully encouraging for the Christian community, and some people in the church begin to feel a bit guilty if they can't match their own story to this one of dramatic conversion. But this is only one possibility.

What, then of 'believing'? To be human is to ask questions. A child who doesn't ask questions may seem a bit odd. A child who asks questions persistently may irritate his parents because they cannot provide an answer! Curiosity may have killed the proverbial cat, but without curiosity humankind would have achieved little.

As they grow older, some people are naturally given to thinking more and more about the deep problems of life – the questions we have touched on elsewhere in this book. Why is humanity so prone to conflict? Why do so many people have to die of hunger? Why did that individual, or that nation, behave in that appalling way? Where did that act of courage come from? What does my own life add up to? What if I had made a different decision all those years ago?

This incessant questioning might itself be rather pointless. But some people really need to sort out these basic ideas in order to feel they have a working principle around which to organize their lives. C. S. Lewis was a passionate atheist who eventually found that without the God in whom he so firmly did *not* believe he couldn't make sense of life. With great reluctance, and after a long struggle, he took the leap of faith and everything fell into place. That will be the kernel of many stories.

And 'belonging'? For many Christians, young and old, it is here that the most resonance is found. All but the most resolutely individualist souls come back, sooner or later, to the question: Where do I fit in? Where do I belong? And this, of course, is about our identity. Who am I?

I remember once going to church – my own church (so it was at the time, long before my ordination), it has to be said – and standing at the back wondering where to sit. I really did not know whereabouts in that company I belonged. It was a very uncomfortable experience. To include that story when I'm talking about belonging might seem rather perverse: fancy admitting that the church failed to provide that sense of belonging when he's trying to persuade us of exactly the opposite. True, of course. But it was clear to me that the question 'Where do I belong?' was a very real and a very important one.

So, for many churchgoers, it is belonging that is most important. Conversation, trivial or deep, with trusted friends of very long standing, collaboration on projects of agreed worth – these things and more are, of course, part of belonging. So too is disagreement, even a measure of dislike, that is held in restraint for the good of everyone. Another part of belonging is the degree to which we retain our own space – we can still be ourselves – while being firmly part of the community. (Some religious communities claim much more space from their adherents than others do.) But most of all, belonging just speaks for itself.

To our three 'b' words there is one more to add: 'becoming'. All your stories will include elements of the first three 'b' words: behaving, belonging and believing. But underlying every life's story is a sense of direction. At the age of 70, you will probably not hold the same views as you held at age 20. You will have acquired some new skills; others you will have lost, either by neglect or because of the ageing process. Life is marked by change, both change outside ourselves and change within ourselves. We are forever 'becoming' someone that we were not and are not yet. Our stories are stories of becoming. Believing, behaving and belonging are elements of that process of becoming, as we discover how to relate to other people in community, to receive from them and give to them.

Probably you can think of other ways of talking about your story. But there is one element that all of them share. Known or not, believed in or not, understood or not, God is the ground of everyone's story.[1] Underlying all of the stories is the love of God in Jesus who proclaimed himself the Way, the Truth and the Life, in perfect response to those three elements: behaving, believing and belonging.

I can hear some voices being raised in mild protest. Am I not being intolerably presumptuous in framing the idea of story in the way that I have just done? Perhaps that is so, but am I (and millions of believers) not entitled to see that framework around all the world's stories, just as a secular atheist is entitled to see a quite different framework? My vision is for a world in which these frameworks can be accepted and evaluated for what they are; a world in which people are not judged simply by the label on the framework which they choose to adopt for their own understanding of the world; a world in which the fundamental ethical watchwords are 'Do no harm', and John Wesley's own dictum, 'Do all the good you can.'

To these four words, perhaps we should add a fifth: 'responding'. It is a sign of a superhero that he 'makes things happen', he is 'proactive' rather than 'reactive'. The word 'responding' on its own is perhaps, therefore, a sign of ineffectiveness. Certainly it isn't in keeping with these go-getting times. But God is the ground of everyone's story. In responding to one another, therefore, we are responding to God. In linking our story with another's or with that of a community, we are learning to identify our story not only with the story of that community, but also with God's story. The Christian faith – like Judaism and Islam – holds God to be prior to everything, including ourselves. Inevitably, therefore, we are responding to what is there already.

By talking in such terms of our relationship with God, we are insisting that ultimately none of us is entirely proactive. To cling to that superhero image is in the end a delusion. God offers us

1 To put it another way, the ground of everyone's story is what God is.

life – and we either accept that gift or reject it. Either way, we are responding to God's offer. The initiative lies not with us, but with God.

One more thing. Behind and woven through our stories are God's stories. In the first book of Samuel one thing stood out as the rise of David was charted: the Lord was with him. He understood where his own roots were planted, and he was faithful to those roots.

11

Modern formulations

This book has been motivated by the desire to encourage people to use the creeds to explore their own faith – ordinary Christians in the pew and especially people who stand outside the Church knowing that they are searching for something and yet are deeply convinced that the Christian Church has nothing to say to them. It may come as a surprise, especially to those familiar only with churches whose strong liturgical traditions require the use of one of the classic creeds to the virtual exclusion of any other, to find that across the churches and indeed across the world, Christian people have been doing just this: writing modern 'creeds' and affirmations of faith.

I can detect two reasons for this. First, the language of the classic creeds is, as we remarked right at the beginning, old-fashioned. It isn't the sort of language you would find in a detective story, a newspaper or a government form. So, many modern credal formulations and affirmations of faith try to update the language, with varying degrees of success. Like all such efforts, they face the twin dangers of being either so contemporary that they themselves date even more quickly than the classic creeds, or of being bland, banal or twee.

There is a second reason, however. Consistently we have referred to the classic creeds – the Apostles', the Nicene and the Athanasian. More strictly, perhaps, we should have referred to them instead as the ecumenical creeds, creeds designed to unify the Church around a particular theological position. It is a tribute to the wisdom and determination of those early churchmen that they were so nearly successful. They did not succeed in uniting the Eastern Church based then in Constantinople with the

Western Church based still in Rome – a division which has lasted to the present day. Their working principle and aim, however, was clear: all Christians are the same; there is one body of Christ. In this they were echoing the words of St Paul in his letter to the church in Ephesus: 'In Christ there is neither Jew nor Greek . . .', and he goes on to list a number of groups which had been kept apart by social custom but are now united in Christ. Nevertheless, the creeds that emerged from their labours represented a search for a common position; they were – to use a modern expression – the work of committees.

We have observed, in our journey, that the world has changed enormously in the centuries since the ecumenical creeds were formulated. It is a world of diversity. Whereas in those far-off days, diversity might be seen only as threat, and unity (if not uniformity) important above all else, today's world reflects and expresses many differences between people. In every imaginable human dimension, people are different, and seek to cherish and express their individuality and group identity while remaining fully committed to the life of this diverse human world. Because communities of faith have for centuries prized their own internal unity above all, coping with diversity presents a particular and acute challenge. It implies a recognition that there are valid ways of understanding life and faith that are different from those to which we are accustomed.

For many deeply committed people of faith, this is extremely hard and even painful. They may have been taught to regard those other ways as simply wrong, to be avoided like the plague. In today's world we have to recognize that different insights, different forms of worship, different words and mental concepts, bring us opportunities for enrichment rather than confrontations that threaten our destruction. The enrichment may take the form of reflecting on our customary usages in the light of the different ways other people do things; on the other hand, it may involve going further – adopting some of those words and customs for ourselves. In terms of all ideologies – social, religious and political – it presents the challenge of seeing diversity as enriching us and our identity, rather than as subtracting from us, or, worse still, denying ourselves.

From a religious perspective, an agenda of embracing diversity will include engagement with other, non-Christian faith communities. Some folk are already involved in such conversation. For others, however, engagement with other Christian communities is problematic enough. It is, for them, a necessary point of departure: this is where we are, where else can we begin?

The life of the mind is no longer dominated by theology; science, economics, transport and environmental concerns now occupy us much more than theology does. A far greater proportion of the population can read and understand complex ideas, and form their own views about them. It may be politically incorrect to say so, but the widespread recognition of human rights has brought with it the belief that everyone's opinion is of equal value, regardless of whether they have taken the trouble to inform themselves about the complex issues involved! That, of course, cannot be undone, though it can be remedied by education.

One consequence of this general move to literacy in a complex world has been the discovery of other fracture-lines through the population, lines that can be exploited by those who seek power and control. I'm thinking of wealth and poverty (bringing in its train the same issues of justice that so aroused the prophets of the Old Testament), ethnicity, gender, sexuality, and so on. In response to this, thoughtful believers, while following this general move to update the language of the creeds, have expressed concerns about the ways in which particular groups are made to feel excluded. Their adaptations of the credal format carry messages about inclusivity which are, strictly, foreign to the thought-world of the ecumenical creeds.

It is very good that people who feel that they are being excluded, not for what they believe but for what they are – women, or gay, or black – are concerned to express their own inner sense of being 'in Christ' by creating formulae and affirmations of faith for liturgical use. Such people are eager to affirm their full belonging to the community of faith, and are trying to work within its customs and structures. The cry seems to be 'We too belong.' Others, who do not feel excluded, may take issue with these new expressions of faith on the grounds that they themselves have no exclusion axe to grind and they cannot see why these new texts are being written or used. The Church has work to do in giving visible effect to Paul's proclamation banishing division from the body of Christ. In fact the emphasis on inclusivity often found in modern texts establishes a rhythm that is absent from the ecumenical creeds unless we scrutinize the text carefully and read between the lines. It *is* possible to find inclusivity in the classic texts, amid the heavily drawn exclusive boundaries, but it is rarely explicit and undeniable. This theme – implicit versus explicit – is one that would form the subject of an interesting study in itself.

In the past few centuries, since the Protestant Reformation and the rise of science, churches and denominations have created Statements of Faith of various kinds, which go far beyond the ecumenical creeds in particular matters. These topics include the authority of the Bible, how people are 'saved', and *who* exactly are saved. Examples include the Thirty-nine Articles of Religion and the great documents of the Reformation.

This brief survey would not be complete without mention of the great stream of anathemas that emerged from the Council of Trent in the sixteenth century. In these we find once again the language of 'Believe this . . . or else' so characteristic of the Athanasian Creed.

In some of these modern official Statements and Declarations we find a reversion to the theme of boundary-marking seen in the Nicene and Athanasian Creeds – exclusiveness once again rearing its head. These credal statements of the second millennium, however, are often marked by a greater degree of harshness than their classic counterparts. There is a tendency to set out very explicitly those beliefs that are not permitted – whereas the classic ecumenical creeds left those prohibitions implicit.

During the course of the twentieth century, many thinkers, writers and poets made attempts to express the content of the faith in modern language. Examples can be found in the Appendix. It is debatable whether these should be referred to as creeds (though some are so designated by their authors), because that would place them alongside the classic ecumenical creeds which are rightly regarded as the Church's deposit of faith, however much we may disagree with them or demand to negotiate with them. These modern formulations do not claim to rival or supplant the classic creeds. Rather, from a variety of perspectives, they constitute part of our negotiation with them, unpacking them and developing their meaning without ever seeking to displace them.

In studying examples of these more modern formulations, you may find it helpful to have in mind a possible classification scheme. Here is one, though it makes no claim to be other than 'possible'.

1 Summary statements of faith, which present the traditional concepts in a very brief form, perhaps in order to meet the needs of infrequent worshippers such as family members at a service of baptism.
2 Modern language statements, which attempt to find modern images and thought-forms in which to express the traditional Christian beliefs.
3 Diversity statements, which express the distinctive viewpoints of particular groups within the worldwide Christian family. These may be ethnic groups who have experienced poverty, marginalization, oppression in one form or other, and who have come to see themselves as defined by those painful experiences. Examples include the poor, black people still enduring the legacy of the slave trade, people with disabilities, women, and lesbian and gay Christians.

This last broad group presents special challenges for shared Christian communication, and particular challenges for me as a married, well-educated white male who, though not rich by some measures, has never felt poor. I cannot put myself in the shoes of *any* of the diverse groups I have mentioned. In even hinting at a possible classification scheme like the above, I run the risk of interposing my own interpretation between a community that feels impelled to express its own faith in a particular way and their intended audience. As so often, the act of observation has disturbed what is being observed.

I am particularly conscious that in including people with disabilities in the list above, I am open to the charge of being dismissive. It is a huge category, a vast group of people who in every way are as diverse as everyone else. To bundle them all together entails severe risk of demeaning all of them – and of course that is far from my aim. This particular instance – the label 'disabled' – does, however, underline my point. Any attempt, however well-intentioned, to embrace diversity by listing definable groups, results almost inevitably in blurring distinctions which individuals hold to be important to them; the outcome can therefore be *ex*clusion rather than *in*clusion.

So, I would encourage you to remember that while a classification scheme might be helpful to you in grasping the overall picture of what is going on, these texts represent voices of people who do not need you to interpret and classify on their behalf; what they ask of you is to listen.

12

The End of the Road?

We are at the end of our journey. Where have we been, what have we seen, what have we done?

The ecumenical creeds attempted to set out in human language some ideas that are in truth beyond the powers of human language to express – to express, that is, in ways that might be seen as comparable with the language we might use, say, to describe a chemical reaction or to explain how aeroplanes fly. Their language is, therefore, necessarily indirect. We have tried to examine the creeds from a metaphorical perspective, as consistently as possible without (this is our hope!) being totally boring about it.

In doing so we have tried to bear in mind the difficulties experienced by some Christian believers when saying the Creed in church. Because the Church so often talks about the Creed as literally true, without explaining the possible ways in which that might or might not be the only option open to us, we believe that people in such a position might feel that they are being required to take it or leave it – take it at face value or leave it alone altogether.

As a result they are left wondering what exactly their faith is. It's a part of them that won't go away, but how can they give it meaningful content? How can they connect it with the meaningful content of other people's faith?

This raises big questions. Does faith have to have meaningful content? Could it be, as a nineteenth-century theologian thought, a feeling inside ourselves? Does it have to be connected with other people at all? How important is 'believing' today, in the sense of holding certain propositions to be true? Clearly, when the ecumenical creeds were composed, such believing was thought to be exceedingly important. It was acceptance of those creeds that constituted a person a Christian, and so constituted the community that accepted them as the Church.

In these postmodern times we might feel less certain about making that claim. People are free to express their beliefs in a variety of ways, and perhaps even to believe in a variety of ways, and still belong together, still claim the same identity. Can a person be a Christian, belong to the church community, be a church member, who finds belief in the Virgin Birth impossible? It may be, as David Harned argues, that the whole traditional Apostles' Creed represents the essential minimum; or perhaps some more concise and economical minimum will suffice. Suppose, however, that propositional believing is not now the 'tie that binds' that it once was? Was it ever the only such tie? What were the others? What alternatives might there be that could hold us together?

There is certainly an argument, put quite strongly by Randall Balmer in his analysis of the Religious Right in the USA,[2] that we must be very cautious about insisting on the literal interpretation of Bible or Creed. To demand, for example, a literal interpretation of propositions about the creation of the world, or human origins, is to concede (perhaps unwittingly) that scientific truth trumps faith truth; in order to be accepted as valid, the truth of faith must be presented as scientific truth, and judged by the same criteria as scientific truth. Like Balmer, I have argued here that this concession has been a grave mistake.

Before we part company to pursue our journeys of faith seeking understanding, it may be worth indulging in some further musing together about the possible directions in which we might go. To the question, 'Was shared belief ever the only criterion for belonging together?', we might suggest the idea of common worship – liturgical forms that travellers would find familiar, regardless of where they happened to be. For centuries the liturgy of the entire Roman Catholic Church was conducted in Latin. The word 'Common' occurs in the Anglican tradition, in the titles of the Book of Common Prayer (BCP) and *Common Worship*. Of these

2 R. H. Balmer, *Thy Kingdom Come: How the Religious Right Distorts the Faith and Threatens America: An Evangelical's Lament*, New York, Basic Books, 2006.

two, the first holds perhaps the greater claim to strict commonality, since it offers no alternatives, while the second offers a bewilderingly wide range of choice, including the time-hallowed BCP texts. The selection may be a once-and-for-all decision by a local church, leading to significant variations between one church and another, but it is a selection from a prescribed list.

The British Methodist Church uses a new Methodist Worship Book (1999) which also contains a great variety of provision. It is differently structured, however, in that nine seasonal Orders for Holy Communion are provided.

Other Christian denominations provide their own worship resources. For some they are mandatory, for others they are merely 'available for use'. Some denominations would find the whole idea of centrally prescribed worship texts entirely alien to their culture. Overall there is immense variety. Yet by and large, Christians of all denominations recognize one another as fellow Christians. It would seem, then, that common worship in the sense of common liturgical texts does not provide the banner around which all Christians rally.

There is one rallying point for the great majority of Christians, however, and it is the fellowship of the Lord's Table, when Christians remember the final meal which Jesus shared with his disciples before he was put to death. Whatever it is called – the Lord's Supper, Holy Communion, the Eucharist or the Mass; however it is interpreted theologically – as memorial or re-enactment; this act of worship is central to the identity of most Christians, embodying as it does both worship and belief, behaving and belonging. Sadly, however, it is not yet a point of true commonality; around some denominations it acts as a barrier to fellowship, not as a welcome into fellowship. And of course in some denominations – the Salvation Army and the Quakers – these issues are irrelevant because in their life together they give no place at all to Sacraments.

Perhaps we are driven to be minimalists, and to recognize that what defines all Christians is their relationship to Jesus, his Spirit within them. Around that central point, however, there is variety and therefore room for disagreement; but there is also space for sharing and discovery and growth.

These questions, and many others, are for your continuing journey – and mine too. All that we have achieved in this book – and I hope and believe it to have been a worthwhile activity – is to open up possibilities for examining our faith from different angles.

So it is not the end of the road at all. Safe journeying!

Appendix

Some Modern Formulations of Belief

This appendix includes samples taken from 20 credal affirmations, which span the range of possible classification set out in Chapter 11: credal summaries, modern creeds and diversity creeds. This means that some are designated 'creeds' which will not at all satisfy some who would wish to reserve that title for the historic ecumenical creeds alone. Except where full permission has been granted, they are presented in the form of extracts together with references to the sources in which they were found.

1 A Methodist Modern Affirmation[1]

This text presents the familiar Trinitarian structure in a modern voice. Like many others among the modern formulations, its emphasis is upon what theologians once called the 'economic Trinity' – that is, upon God's nature inasmuch as it affects human life and experience, in contrast to the 'essential Trinity' – God as God is believed/revealed to be in Godself. It also lays stress upon the ethical commitments (the behaving) involved in believing. The final paragraph runs thus:

> We believe that this faith should manifest itself in the service of love as set forth in the example of our blessed Lord, to the end that the kingdom of God may come upon the earth.
> Amen.

1 Examples 1, 2, and 3 are drawn from a website: http://www.creeds.net/, now (May 2009) being hosted at: http://64.33.81.65/index.htm. The home page of the site attributes this vast collection to Revd Michael Anderson, to whom thanks are due.

2 The Korean Creed

This formulary seems to sit midway between the traditional and the modern. It proclaims belief in 'One God, maker and ruler of all things', and amplifies the familiar belief in forgiveness with these words: 'we believe . . . in the life of love and prayer, and in grace equal to every need'. It also retains a strong emphasis on the final destiny of the world in the 'triumph of righteousness'.

3 An American Presbyterian Creed

Here too, a strong bridge is built between tradition and modernity. The central traditional beliefs of the Church are of course upheld, but there is also a willingness to introduce some modern forms of wording, and to address contemporary issues. One of the interesting features here is the emphasis on community rather than simply on individual salvation. But if a statement of faith is to avoid being simply a 'philosophy of life' it is inevitable that some parts of it will fall strangely on our ears (unless of course we are already Christians). Try as we might, we cannot erase the 'otherness' of language like 'the eternal son of God'. There is here something beyond our human grasp that must nonetheless be reached for. Our beliefs, however 'certain', reflect something we cannot compress into words. The words are never reality itself, but only hints, signs, pointers to another reality, and our search for that reality is the substance of our believing.

4 A Guatemalan Statement of Beliefs[2]

Menchú's text reflects strongly the modern strand of liberation theology. God does not will our suffering; that has been imposed on us by people. Christian commitment involves a refusal to accept as normal these conditions of imposed suffering. The kingdom of God is not 'then' but is firmly 'now', and Christians are charged with responsibility for its planting and nurture. Inner awareness

2 From *I, Rigoberta Menchú* by Rigoberta Menchú, edited by Elisabeth Burgos-Debray, and translated by Ann Wright. Translation © 1984 by Verso.

of God is innate to us humans; it does not require human religious or political hierarchies to teach or guide us.

Arguably this is the most extreme among these credal formulations. God is defined exclusively in relation to human suffering under gratuitous injustice.

5 A Statement of Christian Belief (Presbyterian Church in Canada)[3]

Like that of Menchú, this Statement of Belief expresses a profound concern for justice in the world, under a divine mandate. It reads more as a statement of values rather than of belief, though those values clearly grow out of belief and are derived from biblical sources. But it is less raw, more considered than the Guatemalan text. There is meat here for church convocations to 'get their teeth into' and work out in practical action.

As with the Guatemalan Statement, a wide vision energizes this text. It does not content itself with a few broad generalizations, but sketches the implications of kingdom commitments across a wide range of social concerns.

6 A retro-modern creed[4]

This creed is reproduced with permission from its author, and can speak for itself. It may be that in writing these words 'Dr Ernie' really is writing for himself alone, but I suspect many might be eager to join him.

I believe in Love

I believe in Truth and Justice
as integral to Love
and enabled by Love

3 From Chapter 8, *Living Faith* © The Presbyterian Church in Canada, 1984.

4 Taken from a website entitled 'Radically Happy: A Transformational Bible Blog' and found (in 2009) at: http://2transform.us/2006/06/24/a-retro-modern-creed-take-ii-the-c-of-love/

I believe that Truth, Justice, and Love
are part of the ultimate Reality
that we jointly perceive
with our senses, minds, and feelings

I believe the historical, social, and personal Jesus
manifests that Reality
whom He called Father
and we call God
in His life, death, and resurrection

Which is why I believe in Loving
God with all our heart, soul, mind, and strength
one another as Jesus loves us
our neighbors as ourselves
and even our enemies

I believe in Happiness
based on giving and receiving Love
and expanding the domain of Truth and Justice

I believe in the Hope
that though everything is imperfect
yet nothing is ever in vain
even death itself

I believe in the Failure
of every human creed
including this one
but not of Love itself
or God's own Self
Amen.

7 A Creed (by Bishop David Jenkins)

This, too, is reproduced with permission, and is outstanding in its economy.

God is,
He is as he is in Jesus,
Therefore there is hope.

8 Affirmation of Trinitarian Faith

(Eucharist for Trinity Sunday, written by John Ogden)

I wrote this creed as part of a Eucharist for Trinity Sunday, believing that a mere 'preface to the *Sanctus*' is a somewhat perfunctory acknowledgement of the place of this Christian celebration.

We believe in the unity of all things
created by Your hand alone.

We believe Your Word
proclaimed by prophets,
retold in countless stories,
made flesh in Jesus.

We trust your Spirit
the bearer of new life
for all, for us, for me.

One Church you have called into being.
Our divisions you seek to heal,
so that your kingdom may be seen and celebrated.

We look forward in hope
to the fulfilling of your purpose
and to the wholeness of all creation.

9 A Prayer of Affirmation[5]

(Anna Cory, from *Courage to Love*, page 232)

In her Prayer of Affirmation, Anna Cory does not give us a text to be proclaimed; rather, she offers a simple prayer we might use as a guide in our attempts to understand God through our relationship with God. She reminds us in a most helpful way of the image of God in which we are all made, to honour and love that image in ourselves and others.

10 Statement of Faith

(Ken DeLisle, from *Courage to Love* pages 232–3)

Ken DeLisle speaks for – perhaps from – the heart of the lesbian and gay community. Being often marginalized themselves, it seems to come naturally to him to speak of the marginalized, and ministry to and among them, in his text. This Statement resounds with joy, with emotional connectedness, with living life abundantly, with loving and being loved and so being liberated.

11 We Believe in a Sacred Power

(Susan Kramer, from *Courage to Love*, pages 233, 234)

Kramer's text is clearly not a creed, if by that we mean a coherent set of propositions – or even a story – about God, though she does begin with a 'sacred power within us and around us'. It is of course for her, not me, to interpret her own words (and I commend my own readers to find and study her text and those of Cory and DeLisle and listen to their distinctive voices). But having read and re-read her words, I find here an expression of belief

---

5 This and the following two texts are drawn from G. Duncan, *Courage to Love: An Anthology of Inclusive Worship Material*, London, Darton Longman & Todd, 2002.

that resembles my own, in the same way that a piece of music can be transcribed for other instruments, the result being recognizably related to the original while providing new colours and new insights. She scrupulously avoids the metaphysical language of theology, but speaks very clearly about the transcendent dimension which has pervaded much of this book.

Kramer affirms belief in creativity, justice, dreams, peace, hope, love, potential, celebration, diversity and above all, life!

12 A Creed

(from *Women Included*[6] page 48)

Not surprisingly, given its source, this text affirms the feminine in God and in the beneficent consequences of such affirmation. God is 'mother, source of deep wisdom', our lover, our friend – echoing the proposals of Sallie McFague (in *Models of God*).

As always, this idea of God-as-feminine may strike some as incongruous, perhaps even blasphemous, but it might help if we were more ready to see the idea of God-as-masculine as equally incongruous. But God is envisioned in relational terms – the nourisher, the nurturer, the healer, the revealer of deep mysteries.

There is also here a strong environmental theme. 'We believe in the presence of God in our world . . . whose truth is denied' whenever 'food is withheld, the earth is poisoned, abused or destroyed, people are oppressed, denied dignity and responsibility, tortured or killed.'

13 A Creed

(from *Women Included*, page 49)

Some might describe this as less stridently feminist than the previous one, but still unequivocal in its affirmation of the feminine

6 This and the next text are taken from *Women Included: A Book of Services and Prayers*, London, SPCK, 1991.

as revealing of God's nature. The text is responsive, and focuses attention on the interactions of Jesus with women. He is described as one who 'discussed theology with a woman at a well, who received anointing from a woman at Simon's house, and who rebuked the men guests who scorned her'.

14 A Creed

(from *Bread of Tomorrow*,[7] page 135)

Here we return to the theme of justice and liberation, oppression, martyrdom and the power of the Spirit animating the poor. Typical of its cadences is the following:

> We believe in Jesus Christ,
> friend in suffering,
> companion in the resurrection,
> way of peace.

15 Iona Creed (1)

From the *Iona Abbey Worship Book*, page 74, by Edmund S. P. Jones, and reproduced by permission of Stainer & Bell Ltd, London: www.stainer.co.uk.

This text comes 'from the mainstream' and has a distinctly modern ring. Like some of the other formulations gathered in this appendix, its content is strongly ethical, and like the Prayer of St Francis it counters the life-denying with the life-affirming.

Leader: In the midst of hunger and war
All: We celebrate the promise of plenty and peace.

---

7 J. Morley, *Bread of Tomorrow*, London, SPCK, 1992. Written by Fray Guillermo Chavez, Ecuador, and first published in *Iglesia Solidaria*, June 1987, San Jose, Costa Rica; reprinted in *Latinamerica Press*, 3 September 1987.

Leader:	In the midst of oppression and tyranny
All:	We celebrate the promise of service and freedom.
Leader:	In the midst of doubt and despair
All:	We celebrate the promise of faith and hope.
Leader:	In the midst of fear and betrayal
All:	We celebrate the promise of joy and loyalty.
Leader:	In the midst of hatred and death
All:	We celebrate the promise of love and life.
Leader:	In the midst of sin and decay
All:	We celebrate the promise of salvation and renewal.
Leader:	In the midst of death on every side
All:	We celebrate the promise of the living Christ.
	Amen

Bibliography

Hymns and Psalms, Methodist Publishing House, 1983 (1986).

Women Included: A Book of Services and Prayers, London, SPCK, 1991.

A. Ahmed, *Journey into Islam*, Washington DC, Brookings Institution Press, 2007.

K. Armstrong, *The Battle for God*, London, HarperCollins, 2000.

J. Austen, *Pride and Prejudice: A Novel*, London, T. Egerton, 1813.

M. D. Baker and J. B. Green, *Recovering the Scandal of the Cross: The Atonement in New Testament and Contemporary Contexts*, Downers Grove, Illinois, InterVarsity Press, 2000.

R. H. Balmer, *Thy Kingdom Come: How the Religious Right Distorts the Faith and Threatens America: An Evangelical's Lament*, New York, Basic Books, 2006.

I. G. Barbour, *Myths, Models and Paradigms: The Nature of Scientific and Religious Language*, San Francisco, Harper & Row, 1974.

T. Beattie, *The New Atheists: The Twilight of Reason and the War on Religion*, Maryknoll, NY, Orbis Books, 2008.

D. Brown, *The Da Vinci Code: A Novel*, London; New York, Bantam Press, 2003.

W. Brueggemann, *Isaiah*, Louisville, Ky, Westminster John Knox Press, 1998.

D. Cupitt, *Taking Leave of God*, London, SCM Press, 1980.

R. Dawkins, *The God Delusion*, London, Bantam Press, 2006.

D. C. Dennett, *Breaking the Spell*, London, Allen Lane, 2006.

G. Duncan, *Courage to Love: An Anthology of Inclusive Worship*

Material, London, Darton Longman & Todd, 2002.
J. D. G. Dunn, *Unity and Diversity in the New Testament: An Inquiry into the Character of Earliest Christianity*, London, SCM Press, 1991.
T. Eagleton, *The Illusions of Postmodernism*, Oxford, Blackwell Publishers, 1996 (1997 [printing]).
F. Fukuyama, *The End of History and the Last Man*, London, Hamish Hamilton, 1992.
S. J. Grenz, *A Primer on Postmodernism*, Grand Rapids, Mich.; Cambridge, William B. Eerdmans, 1996.
D. B. Harned, *Creed and Personal Identity: The Meaning of the Apostles' Creed*, Philadelphia, Fortress Press, 1981.
J. Hick, *Evil and the God of Love*, London, Fontana, 1974.
C. Hitchens, *God is not Great: How Religion Poisons Everything*, New York, Twelve, 2007.
M. T. Kelsey, *Myth, History and Faith: The Remythologizing of Christianity*, New York, Paulist Press, 1974.
A. Kohn, *No Contest: The Case Against Competition*, Boston, Houghton Mifflin, 1992.
S. McFague, *Models of God: Theology for an Ecological Nuclear Age*, London, SCM Press, 1987.
A. E. McGrath and J. McGrath, *The Dawkins Delusion: Atheist Fundamentalism and the Denial of the Divine*, Downers Grove, Ill., InterVarsity Press, 2007.
J. Morley, *Bread of Tomorrow*, London, SPCK, 1992.
E. H. Pagels, *The Origin of Satan*, London, Allen Lane, 1996.
T. J. Peters and R. H. Waterman, *In Search of Excellence: Lessons from America's Best-run Companies*, London, Profile, 2004.
D. Z. Phillips, *The Problem of Evil and the Problem of God*, London, SCM Press, 2004.
J. A. T. Robinson, *Honest to God*, London, SCM Press, 1963.
J. W. Rogerson and J. Lieu, *The Oxford Handbook of Biblical Studies*, Oxford, Oxford University Press, 2006.
H. Sharron and M. Coulter, *Changing Children's Minds: Feuerstein's Revolution in the Teaching of Intelligence*, Birmingham, Imaginative Minds, 1996.
J. Swift, J. Chalker and P. Dixon, *Gulliver's Travels; edited by Peter Dixon and John Chalker*, Harmondsworth, Penguin, 1967.

P. Tillich, *The Shaking of the Foundations*, Harmondsworth, Penguin, 1962.
K. Ward, *A Vision to Pursue*, London, SCM Press, 1991.
K. Ward, *Is Religion Dangerous?*, Oxford, Lion, 2006.
G. N. Weber, *I Believe, I Doubt: Notes on Christian Experience*, London, SCM Press, 1998.
A. G. Zornberg, *Genesis: The Beginning of Desire*, Philadelphia, Jewish Publication Society, 1995.

Index